VIEWING SEPTA'S RAIL HERITAGE

Pennsylvania Railroad (PRR) class MP54 electric multiple unit (MU) rail car No. 493 is at the Haws Avenue storage yard in Norristown, Pennsylvania, on October 22, 1960. This was once part of the PRR Schuylkill Branch completed to Norristown, PA, on June 23, 1884, Pottstown, PA, on September 22, 1884, and Reading, PA, on November 24, 1884. With the increase in automobile ownership, plus opening of extension to the Pennsylvania Turnpike, the PRR eliminated the line beyond Manayunk in 1960. (*Kenneth C. Springirth photograph*)

At the 30th Street Yard in Philadelphia, PA, on April 14, 1978, former PRR MP54 electric MU car No. 442 is the first to get the new Southeastern Pennsylvania Transportation Authority (SEPTA) paint scheme. (*Photographer Alfred Gaus Used with permission from Audio Visual Designs [www.audiovisualdesigns.com]*)

VIEWING SEPTA'S RAIL HERITAGE

Beth Anne Keates and Kenneth C. Springirth

FONTHILL

On July 24, 2023, CSX 4,400-horsepower locomotive No. 1982 (originally General Electric [GE] type ES44AH No. 3066 built in 2013 repainted and renumbered 1982 on June 30, 2023) is leading an eastbound CSX freight train parallel to the SEPTA West Trenton Line near the Woodbourne SEPTA Station in Middletown Township, Pennsylvania. This locomotive was the third in a series of heritage locomotives designed and painted at the CSX Waycross Shop in Georgia. The front of the locomotive has the modern CSX colors that transition to the Seaboard System gray, red, and yellow colors. The locomotive was renumbered 1982, which was the year the Seaboard Coast Line absorbed the Louisville & Nashville Railroad. (*Brian A. Keates photograph*)

On top portion of front cover: SEPTA Silverliner V car No. 737 is bringing up the rear of the train on the Manayunk/Norristown Line at the Norristown Elm Street, PA, Station on June 25, 2023. SEPTA ordered 120 of these cars built by Hyundai Rotem. The first car arrived in 2010 with the parts made in South Korea and final assembly in South Philadelphia. All of SEPTA's Silverliner V cars were taken out of service in 2016 and repaired due to fatigue cracks in their trucks. (*Brian A. Keates photograph*)

On bottom portion of front cover: SEPTA Route 15 PCC-II car No. 2327 (originally Car No. 2747 went to Brookville Equipment Corporation for rebuilding on September 9, 2002 and was delivered May 13, 2004) is at Parkside Avenue and 40th Street in Philadelphia on February 3, 2007. Eighteen retired PCC cars were sent to Brookville Equipment Corporation. The first car, No. 2320, was completed and delivered on September 9, 2003. Full trolley car service was restored on Route 15 on September 4, 2005. However, by January 2020, fourteen of the eighteen cars did not pass their internal mechanical inspection, and buses replaced streetcars. On June 16, 2024, eight of the completely rebuilt PCC cars were placed back in service on Route 15. Buses are still being used until the remaining ten PCC cars are restored. (*Kenneth C. Springirth photograph*)

Back cover: Westbound SEPTA Media-Wawa Line train headed by Silverliner IV single end car No. 382 (one of 232 cars built by General Electric Company during 1974–1976) is at the Clifton Aldan Station on July 13, 2023 just before the train crosses the bridge over Springfield Road trolley car tracks of SEPTA's Sharon Hill Line. (*Beth Anne Keates photograph*)

Fonthill Media Inc.
www.fonthillmedia.com
office@fonthillmedia.com

First published 2024

ISBN 978-1-62545-152-1

Typeset in Mrs Eaves XL Serif Narrow
Printed and bound in England

Introduction

The greater Philadelphia, Pennsylvania, area has a rich history of public transit systems. On June 16, 1894, the Ringing Rocks Electric Railway Company opened a 3.75-mile electric trolley line from Pottstown north to Ringing Rocks Park. The Oley Railway opened a line from Reading to Boyertown on May 23, 1902. Roxborough, Chestnut Hill & Norristown Traction Company began through Roxborough–Norristown trolley service on October 20, 1894. Through Chestnut Hill–Pottstown trolley service began by the Schuylkill Valley Traction Company on June 23, 1905. Created on May 29, 1906, the Boyertown & Pottstown Railway Company began trolley service between Boyertown and Pottstown on May 28, 1908. The Schuylkill Valley Traction Company became part of the Reading Transit & Light Company on March 28, 1913. Through Chestnut Hill–Boyertown trolley service began on December 18, 1916. The first trolley line to be converted to bus operation in this area was the Boyertown to Pottstown line, which made its last trolley run on August 21, 1927. Roxborough and Manayunk trolley service ended on December 12, 1931. Chestnut Hill–Norristown line ended trolley service on December 13, 1931. Trolley service west of Collegeville ended on January 21, 1932. Service from Reading to Boyertown ended in July 1932. The reorganized Schuylkill Valley Lines converted the remaining trolley lines to bus operation on September 10, 1933. SEPTA acquired Schuylkill Valley Lines on March 1, 1976 and established its Frontier Division, which restructured the former Schuylkill Valley bus routes on March 7, 1977.

The Southeastern Pennsylvania Transportation Authority (SEPTA) according to the SEPTA Fact Sheet 2019 (Fiscal year ended June 30, 2019) had thirteen lines in its regional rail system that carried 34,191,260 passengers with a fleet of 396 cars, of which 342 cars were used in peak hours; eight lines in its light rail system (streetcar) with six in the City of Philadelphia and two in Delaware County that carried 24,720,500 passengers with a fleet of 159 cars, of which 120 were used in peak hours; Norristown High Speed Line (NHSL) one line that carried 3,104,753 passengers with a fleet of twenty-six cars, of which nineteen were used in peak hours; Market-Frankford Subway Elevated Line (MFSE) one line that carried 51,953,426 passengers with a fleet of 218 cars, of which 156 were used in peak hours; and the Broad Street Subway (BSS) that carried 35,474,365 passengers with a fleet of 125 cars, of which 112 were used in peak hours.

Reading Railroad commuter car No. 9103 is part of a two-car train at Wayne Junction in the Nicetown neighborhood of Philadelphia on February 22, 1969. This car was one of thirty-eight cars completely rebuilt during 1963–1965 by the Reading Railroad with new seat cushions, fluorescent lighting, and better ventilation. They became known as "Blueliners" because of their distinctive white and blue paint scheme. (*Kenneth C. Springirth photograph*)

This map shows the extensive connectivity by railroad and interurban trolley lines with emphasis on the former Reading Railroad Lansdale/Doylestown Line now operated by SEPTA and the unique former Lehigh Valley Transit (LVT) Liberty Bell Line, connecting Allentown through Lansdale and Norristown via Philadelphia & Western Railroad to 69th Street Terminal plus the LVT Chestnut Hill Branch that connected directly with Philadelphia Transportation Company Route 23 at Chestnut Hill.

Lansdale, Pennsylvania, is the location of Lehigh Valley Transit (LVT) car No. 1000 in 1950. This originally was Cincinnati & Lake Erie Railroad (C&LE) car No. 125 that was built in 1930 by the Cincinnati Car Company. LVT purchased eleven aluminum-construction C&LE cars that had operated daily service on a 260-mile run between Cincinnati via Toledo to Detroit and a 315-mile-long run from Cincinnati via Toledo to Cleveland. Each car received extensive exterior and interior renovations by LVT shop personnel, including a picador cream-lacquered car body, mountain ash scarlet pyramid tapered from the front bumper to a peak near the roof above the front center window, and "Liberty Bell Limited" lettered in scarlet above the side windows. (*Photographer Eugene Van Dusen Used with permission from Audio Visual Designs [www.audiovisualdesigns.com]*)

On April 1, 2021, SEPTA high-speed electric passenger 1,340-horsepower type ACS-64 locomotive No. 905 is at the Malvern, Pennsylvania, Station waiting for departure time on the SEPTA Paoli–Thorndale Line. Weighing 215,537 pounds, this was one of thirteen new locomotives (Nos. 901–913) ordered by SEPTA in July 2015 and designed and manufactured by Siemens Mobility at its factory in Florin, California, near Sacramento. SEPTA's first ACS-64 was delivered on December 14, 2017, and the order was increased to fifteen locomotives. (*Andrew L. Keates photograph*)

An eastbound Amtrak passenger train, headed by Siemens locomotive No. 616, is powering an eastbound passenger train past the Whitford, Chester County, Pennsylvania, Station. This is one of seventy Siemens type ACS-64 electric locomotives (Nos. 600–670) that were delivered beginning February 2014 until August 2016. Amtrak trains currently do not stop at this station; however, SEPTA Paoli/Thorndale trains serve this station. Directly above the station is the former Pennsylvania Railroad bridge built in 1906 that was used for freight trains and was abandoned by Conrail in 1989. (*Andrew L. Keates photograph*)

On April 20, 2020, Pennsylvania Northwestern Railroad diesel electric locomotive No. 8212 (3,900-horsepower six-axle General Electric [GE] type C39-8 built in August 1986 for Consolidated Rail Corporation [Conrail] as No. 6021) is powering a general manifest train through Lansdale, Pennsylvania. That locomotive is the last operating C39-8 locomotive in North America. The overhead wire is for SEPTA's electrified Lansdale/Doylestown Line. (*Andrew L. Keates photograph*)

1

Philadelphia Regional Rail

By the late 1950s, commuter service requiring many passenger cars, many employees to operate the cars and station sites, plus considerable track maintenance on track that had heavy usage in the morning and afternoon rush-hour period had an adverse effect on profitability for both the Pennsylvania Railroad (PRR) and Reading Company (RDG). When the Philadelphia suburbs were small towns, people lived close enough to a train station to walk to and from the trains. As the suburbs grew, fields disappeared, and with a decline in the cost of buying an automobile, more commuters purchased automobiles. Faced with the possible loss of railroad commuter service, the City of Philadelphia in 1958 enacted the Philadelphia Passenger Service Improvement Corporation (PSIC) which was a partnership with the PRR and RDG to subsidize service on the Chestnut Hill East Line and Chestnut Hill West Line. The subsidy program was expanded in 1962 in a five-county suburban area under the Southeastern Pennsylvania Transportation Compact (SEPACT). In 1966, SEPTA began subsidizing commuter lines of the Pennsylvania Railroad and Reading Company. On February 1, 1968, the Pennsylvania Railroad merged with the New York Central forming the Penn Central Transportation Company (Penn Central), which went bankrupt on June 21, 1970. The Reading Company filed for bankruptcy on November 23, 1971. Consolidated Rail Corporation (Conrail) took over railroad-related assets and operation of the Penn Central and Reading Company on April 1, 1976. Conrail operated commuter rail services under contract to SEPTA until January 1, 1983 when SEPTA took over operation.

Six of Philadelphia's regional rail lines were originally operated by the Pennsylvania Railroad (PRR) and used Philadelphia's downtown Suburban Station located at 16th and JFK Boulevard as the underground terminus. Six were originally operated by the Reading Railroad and used an elevated approach above city streets into downtown Philadelphia's Reading Terminal located on Market Street at 12th Streets. Ground breaking occurred on June 22, 1978, for the Center City Commuter Connection (CCCC) proposed by R. Damon Childs, junior land planner, of the Philadelphia City Planning Commission. The $330 million tunnel project also included construction of the Market East Station on Market Street between 10th and 12th Streets in downtown Philadelphia. SEPTA trains on the former PRR lines began using the new 1.8-mile four-track tunnel from Suburban Station to Market East Station on November 12, 1984. Reading Terminal (replaced by Market East Station) handled its last train (a special train from Lansdale) on November 6, 1984. Final track connections were completed four days later so that former Reading Railroad commuter trains now used the CCCC Tunnel to and from Center City via the Market East Station. On September 4, 2014, SEPTA announced that Market East Station was renamed Jefferson Station after Jefferson Health (whose Thomas Jefferson University Hospital is located a few blocks from the station) purchased the naming rights.

Most inbound trains from one line continue on as outbound trains on another line. All trains on the Cynwyd Line terminate at Suburban Station on 16th Street and JFK Boulevard in Philadelphia.

SEPTA Airport Line

SEPTA's Airport Line (which consisted of new construction, a reconstructed former Pennsylvania Railroad industrial branch, and a former Reading Company freight branch) opened on April 28, 1985. After the line leaves Gray 30th Street Station (which on April 8, 2024 was renamed Drexel Station at 30th Street), stops are made at Penn Medicine, Eastwick, and four stops at the Philadelphia International Airport: Terminal A, Terminal B, Terminal C and D, and Terminal E and F. The April 16, 2023 Airport Line schedule shows most Mondays through Fridays (except major holidays) trains are through routed with the Warminster Line and Fox Chase Line and alternate between terminating in Warminster and Fox Chase. Most weekend trains are through routed with the Warminster Line and alternate between terminating in Glenside and Warminster.

SEPTA Chestnut Hill East Line

SEPTA's Chestnut Hill East Line serves the northwestern Philadelphia neighborhoods of Germantown, Mount Airy, and Chestnut Hill. This line began as the Philadelphia, Germantown & Norristown Railroad (incorporated on April 5, 1831) which opened from Philadelphia to Germantown on June 6, 1832. Plans to build north from Germantown to Norristown were changed to a different route that branched off the existing line at what is now 16th Street Junction. Germantown remained the northernmost station on the branch until 1854 when the Chestnut Hill Railroad leased by the Philadelphia, Germantown & Norristown Railroad extended the line 4 miles to Chestnut Hill, which opened on December 1, 1854. The

Philadelphia & Reading Railroad (later Reading Company) leased the Philadelphia, Germantown & Norristown Railroad on December 1, 1870. This line was electrified by the Reading Company on February 5, 1933. With the Reading Company in bankruptcy in 1976, the Chestnut Hill East Line was conveyed to Conrail and later SEPTA. On April 2, 2020, service on this line was suspended due to the COVID-19 pandemic. Service resumed on June 28, 2020. According to the April 16, 2023 Chestnut Hill East Line schedule, most trains are through routed with service to the Trenton, New Jersey, Transit Center.

SEPTA Chestnut Hill West Line

SEPTA's Chestnut Hill West Line runs roughly parallel to the Chestnut Hill East Line with some stations less than half a mile apart. The Philadelphia, Germantown & Chestnut Hill Railroad opened the line on June 1, 1884. Electrified on March 30, 1918, it was operated by the Pennsylvania Railroad until 1968. On February 1, 1968, it was operated by Penn Central Transportation Company (Penn Central), later Conrail, and SEPTA took over in 1983. From June 26, 1987 until December 17, 1989, rail service ended at Allen Lane, with shuttle buses serving St. Martin's, Highland, and Chestnut Hill West stations because the original iron Cresheim Valley bridge built in 1884 was replaced by a $7.6 million steel bridge funded by the Urban Mass Transportation Administration. On April 9, 2020, Chestnut Hill West service was suspended due to reduced ridership because of the COVID-19 pandemic plus AMTRAK construction along the Northeast Corridor that was used for part of the Chestnut Hill West Line. Chestnut Hill West Line Monday to Friday service was restored on March 8, 2021 and weekend service was restored on December 19, 2021. As shown by the April 16, 2023 SEPTA Chestnut Hill West line schedule, certain Monday to Friday trips terminate at Temple University while some terminate at Miquon, Chestnut Hill East, and West Trenton. Most Saturday, Sunday, and major holiday trips terminate at West Trenton.

SEPTA Cynwyd Line

SEPTA's 6.1-mile Cynwyd Line is a shortened segment of the former Pennsylvania Railroad's Schuylkill Branch that operated from Philadelphia to Pottstown. Electrified service began between Philadelphia and Haws Avenue in Norristown on June 20, 1930. Passenger service ended between Manayunk and Norristown on October 29, 1960. In 1980, service was extended from Manayunk to Ivy Ridge; however, service beyond Cynwyd was discontinued on May 27, 1986, making the Cynwyd Line SEPTA's shortest line. Silverliner V rail cars made their first revenue run on October 29, 2010 on the Cynwyd Line. Final Silverliner II and III cars made their last revenue run on June 29, 2012 on the Cynwyd Line. A staff shortage caused by the COVID-19 pandemic closed the line on April 9, 2020. Limited service resumed on September 7, 2021. The August 21, 2022 SEPTA Cynwyd Line (Cynwyd-Suburban Station) schedule showed six trips Monday through Fridays (except major holidays).

SEPTA Fox Chase Line

SEPTA's Fox Chase Line had its beginning as the Philadelphia & Montgomery County Railroad chartered on April 2, 1860; however, on January 29, 1873, the name was changed to Philadelphia, Newtown & New York Railroad, which was leased by the Pennsylvania Railroad on October 22, 1873. The Philadelphia to Fox Chase portion opened on June 14, 1876 and Fox Chase to Newtown opened on February 4, 1878 followed by the Philadelphia & Reading Railroad leasing the line on November 12, 1879. Effective December 31, 1945, the Philadelphia, Newtown & New York Railroad was merged into the Reading Company. The City of Philadelphia funded electrification of the line from Philadelphia to Fox Chase (last station within Philadelphia city limits), which was completed on September 29, 1966. Diesel operation continued from Fox Chase to Newtown. With the Reading Company in bankruptcy, the Newtown Line was conveyed to SEPTA, which suspended diesel service to Newtown on July 1, 1981 as part of a system-wide discontinuation of non-electrified service. SEPTA operated a version of diesel service known as the Fox Chase Rapid transit Line from October 5, 1981 to when it was finally suspended on January 18, 1983. The April 16, 2023 SEPTA Fox Chase schedule shows most Monday to Friday trips are through routed to the Airport, and all Saturday, Sunday, and major holiday trips are through routed to Wawa.

SEPTA Lansdale/Doylestown Line

SEPTA's Lansdale/Doylestown Line began with the incorporation of the Philadelphia, Easton & Water Gap Railroad on April 8, 1852. Construction began on June 16, 1853, and the company changed its name to North Penn Railroad (NPRR) on October 3, 1853. The railroad opened from Front and Willow Streets in Philadelphia to Gwynedd on July 2, 1855. NPRR chief surveyor Philip Lansdale Fox established the location of the junction for the line to Doylestown and via Lansdale the NPRR opened to Doylestown on October 7, 1855. The NPRR reached Bethlehem on July 7, 1857 where the NPRR interchanged with the Lehigh Valley Railroad. Electrified service between Philadelphia and Hatboro, Lansdale, Doylestown, and West Trenton began on July 26, 1931. Rail passenger service to Bethlehem declined as automobile ownership increased along with the opening of the Pennsylvania Turnpike Northeast Extension. Lansdale station was once an important transfer point between electric and rail diesel car (RDC) service north to places such as Quakertown, Bethlehem, and Allentown. RDC service on the Bethlehem line ended in 1981. The January 8, 2023 Lansdale/Doylestown schedule shows some Monday to Friday trains are through routed to Marcus Hook, Chestnut Hill West, Wilmington, and Wawa. Saturday trains are through routed to Malvern and Thorndale. Sunday and major holiday trains are mostly through routed to Malvern.

SEPTA Manayunk/Norristown Line

SEPTA's Manayunk/Norristown Line began with the Philadelphia, Germantown & Norristown Railroad (PG&N) opening a 6-mile line from Philadelphia to Germantown on June 6, 1832. The company changed its original intention of building from Germantown to Norristown and instead built west from 16th Street Junction in North Philadelphia, reaching Manayunk on October 18, 1834 and Norristown on August 15, 1835. The PG&N had a bridge built (by the Swedes Ford Bridge Company) over the Schuylkill River completed in 1851 connecting Norristown and Bridgeport, Pennsylvania. That bridge, opened in 1851, made possible a connection with the Philadelphia & Reading Railroad which leased the Philadelphia Germantown & Norristown Railroad. Electrified service to Norristown began on February 5, 1933. Service on the line was suspended on April 9, 2020 due to the COVID-19 pandemic. On June 28, 2020, service was restored. Hurricane Ida remnants on September 1–2, 2021 caused severe flooding along the Schuylkill River, with the Manayunk/Norristown Line between Miquon and Norristown flooded and damaged. Service between Center City, Philadelphia, and Spring Mill resumed on September 7, 2021, and service along the entire length of the line to Norristown resumed on September 13, 2021. The August 21, 2022 Manayunk/Norristown schedule shows most Monday to Friday trains are through routed to Wawa plus one to Bryn Mawr and two to Chestnut Hill West. On Saturdays, Sundays, and major holidays, most trains are through routed to Wilmington and one to Trenton Transit Center.

SEPTA Media/Wawa Line

SEPTA's Media/Wawa Line was originally built by the West Chester & Philadelphia Railroad (WC&P) on November 15, 1853, extended service to Media on October 19, 1854, Wawa in 1857, and to West Chester on November 11, 1858. The WC&P merged with the Philadelphia & Baltimore Central Railroad (P&BC) in 1881, and both were controlled by the Pennsylvania Railroad. Wawa Station was originally known as the Baltimore Central Junction Station (northern terminus of the P&BC and the line later known as the Octoraro Branch). Electrified service began on December 2, 1928. Pennsylvania Railroad and New York Central Railroad merged into Penn Central on February 1, 1968. After the Market Street Station in West Chester, Pennsylvania, Station was demolished in 1968, Penn Central constructed a small shelter initially named Nields Street and later became West Chester University Station. The last day of passenger service was September 18, 1986, with the line cut back to Elwyn, Pennsylvania. Work on restoring a 3.5-mile section of the line from Elwyn to Wawa began in 2018 with new track, catenary including support structures, a new station at Wawa, Pennsylvania, with a park and ride facility, replacement of the railroad bridge over U.S. Highway Route 1 (Baltimore Pike), construction of a new traffic intersection and access road connecting Wawa Station with U.S. Highway Route 1, replacement of the rail bridge over Lungren Road, a new rail yard at Lenni, and a 600-car parking area. The line opened August 21, 2022, and the revised August 23, 2022 Media/Wawa schedule shows most Monday to Friday trains are through routed to Elm Street, with three to West Trenton, one to Glenside, one to Chestnut Hill East, and one to Warminster. On Saturdays, Sundays, and major holidays, most trains are through routed to Fox Chase.

SEPTA Paoli/Thorndale Line

SEPTA's Paoli/Thorndale Line traces its beginning when the state of Pennsylvania authorized construction of the Philadelphia & Columbia Railroad (P&C) on March 24, 1828. The first section opened from Philadelphia to Paoli on September 20, 1832. Beginning at the corner of Broad and Vine Streets in Philadelphia, the line crossed the Schuylkill River below Peter Island. The Belmont Inclined Plane hauled cars up a half-mile 7-percent grade on the high ground above the river. Heading west the line was on level ground and descended onto the Chester Valley to Lancaster and to Columbia where another inclined plane let the cars down to the canal basin by the Susquehanna River where the Pennsylvania Canal began. On October 7, 1834, the Philadelphia to Columbia Railroad officially opened. The P&C was part of the Main Line of Public Works (a system of railroads and canals that connected Philadelphia with Pittsburgh) that was purchased by the Pennsylvania Railroad on June 24, 1857. By the 1870s, the communities along the Pennsylvania Railroad mainline from Philadelphia to Paoli developed into the upscale "Mainline." Electrified commuter service between Philadelphia and Paoli began on September 11, 1915. SEPTA's Paoli/Thorndale Line is part of the Keystone Corridor which handles Amtrak passenger trains. On November 22, 1999, SEPTA extended the Paoli Line west to Thorndale, Pennsylvania. The April 16, 2023 Paoli/Thorndale Line schedule shows certain Monday to Friday trains are through routed to Doylestown, Lansdale, Neshaminy Falls, West Trenton, Glenside, and Norristown Transit Center. On Saturdays, Sundays, and major holidays, certain trains are through routed to Doylestown and Lansdale. There is no Sunday holiday service to Thorndale, Downingtown, Whitford, and Exton.

SEPTA Trenton Line

SEPTA's Trenton Line is part of the middle leg of Amtrak's Northeast Corridor. Camden & Amboy Railroad (first US railroad to use wooden ties and T-section rails) completed their line in New Jersey from Bordentown to South Amboy and carried their first passengers via horsecars on December 17, 1832. Philadelphia & Trenton Railroad (P&T) opened their line from Philadelphia to Trenton in 1834. According to the *Centennial History of the Pennsylvania Railroad 1846–1946* by George H. Burgess and Miles C. Kennedy: "Through service to Philadelphia began on January 1, 1839 with the inauguration of two schedules a day in each direction. The Morning Line left the foot of Liberty Street, New York at 9:00 A.M. and arrived in Philadelphia in season to take the 3 P.M. Train for Baltimore." The Connecting Railway Company, incorporated May 15, 1863, in June 1867 completed a 6.75-mile line connecting Frankford Junction on the Philadelphia & Trenton Railroad with Mantua Junction on the Pennsylvania Railroad later known as Zoo interlock. The Pennsylvania Railroad leased the Philadelphia & Trenton Railroad (P&T) on June 30, 1871, and began operating it on December 1, 1871. Electrified service between Philadelphia and Trenton began on June 29, 1930. The April 16, 2023 Trenton Line schedule shows certain Monday to Friday trains are through routed to Chestnut Hill East. On Saturdays, Sunday, and major holidays, certain trains are through routed to Chestnut Hill East and one train is through routed to Norristown Transit Center.

SEPTA Warminster Line

SEPTA's Warminster Line was originally built by the North East Pennsylvania Railroad (a subsidiary of North Pennsylvania Railroad) from the North Pennsylvania Railroad's main line at Glenside and completed north of Hatboro to the Bucks/Montgomery County line on December 18, 1872. A further extension to Hartsville opened on November 9, 1874. From 1879 until 1976, this was part of the Reading Company which electrified the portion between Glenside and Hatboro on July 26, 1931. Passenger service beyond Hatboro ended on June 7,1952. The Reading, with SEPTA's support, extended electrification from Hatboro to Warminster on July 29, 1974, and SEPTA owns the line. The January 8, 2023 Warminster Line schedule shows most trains are through routed to the Airport, one train is through routed to Thorndale, and one train is through routed to Newark, Delaware. On Saturdays, Sundays, and major holidays, all trains are through routed to the Airport.

SEPTA West Trenton Line

SEPTA's West Trenton Line north of the split at Jenkintown to the Delaware River was built by the North Pennsylvania Railroad opened on May 1, 1876. The New Jersey section via West Trenton, New Jersey, was built by the Delaware & Bound Brook Railroad. Both the Reading Company and Baltimore & Ohio Railroad freight and passenger trains used the Philadelphia via West Trenton, New Jersey, line to reach New York City. Electrified service was opened by the Reading Railroad to West Trenton, New Jersey, on July 26, 1931. CSX gained control of the line from West Trenton to Hillsborough in 1999. The April 16, 2023 West Trenton Line schedule shows certain Monday to Friday trains are through routed to Malvern, Media, Newark Delaware, Chestnut Hill West, and Thorndale. On Saturday, Sunday, and major holidays, most trains are through routed to Chestnut Hill West and one to the Airport.

SEPTA Wilmington/Newark Line

SEPTA's Wilmington/Newark Line began on April 2, 1831 when the General Assembly of Pennsylvania chartered the Philadelphia & Delaware County Railroad Company (P&DC). On January 18, 1832, the State of Delaware chartered the Wilmington & Susquehanna Railroad to build from Wilmington, Delaware, to the Maryland state line. On March 5, 1832, the State of Maryland chartered Baltimore & Port Deposit Railroad (B&PD) to build from Baltimore to the western bank of the Susquehanna River. On March 12, 1832, Delaware & Maryland Railroad (D&M) was chartered to build from Port Deposit north to Delaware State Line. On March 14, 1836, the P&DC changed its name to Philadelphia Wilmington & Baltimore Railroad Company PW&B). On July 4, 1836, the PW&B began building a bridge across the Schuylkill River. The D&M merged into the Wilmington & Susquehanna Railroad Company on April 18, 1836. The PW&B opened service from Wilmington to Gray's Ferry (at that time, a few miles south of the city limits) on January 15, 1838. Passengers getting off the train at Gray's Ferry were taken by omnibus into Philadelphia. The three remaining state-chartered railroads merged on February 12, 1838 to form Philadelphia, Wilmington & Baltimore Railroad Company (PW&B). In December 1938, the PW&B completed its bridge across the Schuylkill River at Gray's Ferry. Trains operated from downtown Philadelphia to downtown Baltimore using a steam railroad ferry to cross the Susquehanna River. In November 1866, a wooden bridge was built across the Susquehanna River creating a continuous connection between Philadelphia and Baltimore. On April 1, 1886, the Pennsylvania Railroad obtained complete control of the PW&B. Electrified service opened on September 30, 1928 between Philadelphia and Wilmington. When SEPTA took over on January 1, 1983, commuter rail service to Delaware was discontinued, and Marcus Hook, Pennsylvania, became the southern terminus. In 1989, service was extended south to Wilmington, Delaware, adding stops in Claymont in 1991, Newark in 1997, and Churchmans Crossing in 2000. The April 16, 2023 Wilmington/Newark Line schedule shows certain Monday to Friday trains are through routed to Doylestown, one train is through routed to Norristown Transit Center, and one train is through routed to Lansdale. On Saturday, Sunday, and major holidays, all trains are through routed to Elm Street (793 Markley Street, Norristown).

Above: SEPTA commuter car No. 364 is making a stop at the Eastwick Station (in Eastwick neighborhood of Philadelphia) on the Airport Line heading to Center City, Philadelphia, on January 20, 2016. This is one of 232 Silverliner IV cars designed plus built by General Electric and delivered between 1973 and 1976. These cars allowed for the retirement of most of the Reading multiple unit cars and the Pennsylvania Railroad MP54 cars. (*Michael Pearson photograph*)

Right: SEPTA Regional Rail operates thirteen commuter lines in the Philadelphia metropolitan area. Twelve of these lines serve the three downtown Philadelphia Stations Gray 30th Street, Suburban Station, and Jefferson Station. The Cynwyd Line serves Gray 30th Street Station and Suburban Station. Based on American Public Transportation Association Commuter Rail Public Transportation Ridership Report Fourth Quarter 2022, SEPTA ranks sixth in the United States for the year 2022 commuter ridership as follows: 1 New York–MTA Long Island Railroad 70,342,700, 2 New York–MTA Metro-North Railroad 52,197,600, 3 Newark–New Jersey Transit Corp 45,838,200, 4 Chicago–Metra 23,726,400, 5 Boston–Massachusetts Bay Transportation Authority 19,000,800, and 6 Philadelphia–SEPTA 15,907,400.

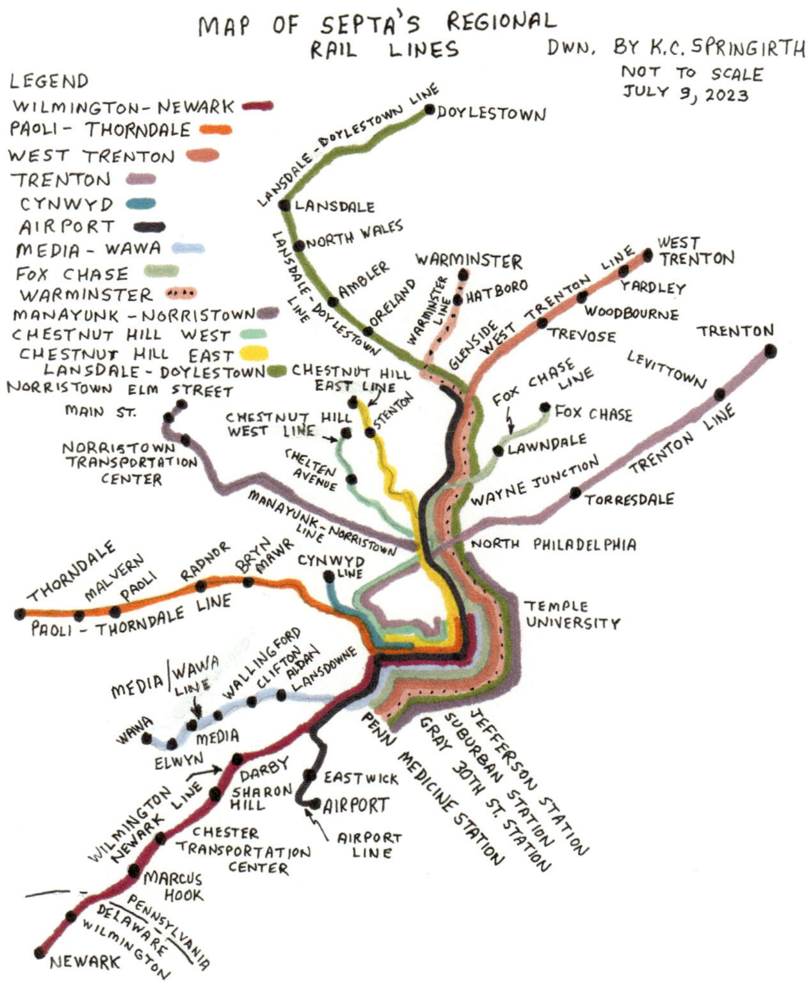

On August 1, 2023, SEPTA Silverliner IV car No. 385 leads a train from William H. Gray III 30th Street Station into the Chestnut Hill East Station, which was rebuilt by the Reading Railroad in 1931. (*Brian A. Keates photograph*)

SEPTA Silverliner IV car No. 153 brings a train into the Sedgwick Station on its way to the Chestnut Hill East Station on August 1, 2003. This station has low-level platforms with open shelters. (*Brian A. Keates photograph*)

On a bright August 1, 2023, SEPTA Silverliner IV car No. 372 is at the rear of a commuter train that is leaving Sedgwick Station on its way to the Chestnut Hill East Station. (*Brian A. Keates photograph*)

Chestnut Hill West Line Station, in the Chestnut Hill neighborhood of Philadelphia, is the location of Silverliner IV car No. 172 waiting for departure time for its next trip to Center City, Philadelphia, on August 1, 2023. This line had its beginning with the January 2, 1883 incorporation of the Philadelphia, Germantown & Chestnut Hill Railroad, which, completed by 1884, was the basis of SEPTA's Chestnut Hill West Line. (*Brian A. Keates photograph*)

On a cloudy bright August 1, 2023, Silverliner car No. 361 is at the Chestnut Hill West Station. It was 105 years ago when the March 23, 1918 *Harrisburg Telegraph* newspaper reported: "Electric train service began yesterday when the Pennsylvania Railroad sent a test train over the line." Electrification of the line (through Germantown to Chestnut Hill West Station) cost over $1.5 million. The newspaper article noted: "The construction included 150 miles of copper wire and erection of 230 steel poles." (*Brian A. Keates photograph*)

SEPTA Silverliner car No. 361 is at Carpenter Station on the Chestnut Hill West Line ready to continue a trip to downtown Philadelphia on August 1, 2023. Delivery of the Silverliner IV cars allowed SEPTA to replace most of the pre-war Pennsylvania Railroad MP54 fleet. (*Brian A. Keates photograph*)

On May 30, 2019, Silverliner IV car No. 282, on the Cynwyd Line, is at the SEPTA Bala Station, a community in Lower Merion Township, Pennsylvania. The approximate 6-mile Cynwyd Line is SEPTA's shortest line, with the lowest ridership, and is the second shortest United States regional rail line. The shortest U.S. regional rail line is New Jersey's 2.7-mile Princeton Branch. (*Michael Pearson photograph*)

SEPTA Silverliner IV car No. 411 is at the Bala Station on June 3, 2015 on the Cynwyd Line, which is a small surviving segment of the Pennsylvania Railroad's Schuylkill Branch that connected Philadelphia to Pottsville. Electrified service began between Philadelphia and Haws Avenue in Norristown on June 20, 1930. Passenger service ended from Manayunk to Norristown on October 29, 1960. Service beyond Cynwyd ended on May 27, 1986 because of poor track, plus concerns about the Manayunk Bridge over the Schuylkill River. (*Michael Pearson photograph*)

On August 26, 2016, SEPTA Silverliner IV car No. 165 is waiting for departure time at the Fox Chase Station terminus of the Fox Chase Line in the Fox Chase neighborhood of Philadelphia. (*Kenneth C. Springirth photograph*)

Cheltenham Station, in the Burholme neighborhood of Northeast Philadelphia on the Fox Chase Line, is the location of SEPTA Silverliner IV car No. 172 on July 22, 2023. (*Brian A. Keates photograph*)

Pennsylvania Northeastern Railroad diesel electric locomotive No. 5342 (built by Electro Motive Division of General Motors [EMD] 3,000-horsepower type SD40-2W [Canadian version of an SD40-2] originally Canadian National Railway No. 5342 built in 1980) is leading a freight train past the Lansdale train station on April 18, 2020. Back in 2011, this railroad took over freight operation on 56 miles of SEPTA-owned lines from Newtown Junction to Telford, Pennsylvania (PA); Lansdale to Doylestown, PA; Glenside to Ivyland, PA; Jenkintown to Neshaminy, PA; and a portion of the Stony Creek line in Montgomery County, PA. (*Andrew L. Keates photograph*)

On April 18, 2020, Pennsylvania Northeastern Railroad diesel electric locomotive No. 8212 (GE 3,900-horsepower type C39-8 originally built in August 1986 as Conrail No. 6021) is powering a freight train past the historic Lansdale, PA, train station (designed by architect Louis Caron Hickman of Philadelphia) which has a plaque that reads: "P&R Railway, Lansdale Passenger Station, Built 1902, Has Been Placed On The National Register of Historic Places, by The United States Department Of The Interior." That listing occurred on December 13, 2021. This station is an example of Beaux-Arts architecture characterized by symmetry and a grand entrance. (*Andrew L. Keates photograph*)

SEPTA Silverliner V car No. 803 built by Hyundai Rotem (car body shells made in South Korea and final assembly completed in South Philadelphia) with an advertising wrap is in a train of cars at the SEPTA Lansdale, Pennsylvania, Station on the Lansdale/Doylestown Line awaiting departure time on June 4, 2023. Over the July 4, 2016 holiday weekend, SEPTA took the entire 120 Hyundai Rotem car fleet, built at a cost of $274 million, out of service because equalizer beams on the cast-steel truck frame had vertical fatigue cracks. In a September 12, 2016 SEPTA news release, it was noted that "SEPTA has temporarily sidelined 18 Silverliner V cars that had been repaired by the manufacturer and were recently returned to service, or had been readied for service. A minor design modification will be made to the foot that supports the new equalizer beam at both ends." *(Brian A. Keates photograph)*

On a beautiful June 4, 2023, SEPTA Silverliner V car No. 728 built by Hyundai Rotem is at the Lansdale Station ready for the next run to downtown Philadelphia on June 4, 2023. Hyundai Rotem's South Philadelphia plant closed in 2018. *(Brian A. Keates photograph)*

SEPTA Silverliner IV car No. 337 is the rear car on the train leaving the Lansdale Station on June 4, 2023 heading for Center City, Philadelphia. Lansdale is a borough in Montgomery County, Pennsylvania. (*Brian A. Keates photograph*)

On June 4, 2023, SEPTA Silverliner IV car No. 299 is waiting for departure time at Doylestown Station to make its run to Philadelphia. This is the last station on SEPTA's Lansdale/Doylestown Line. Doylestown is a borough and county seat of Bucks County, Pennsylvania. (*Brian A. Keates photograph*)

At the Doylestown, Pennsylvania, Station, SEPTA Silverliner IV car No. 299 is ready to lead the train on the Lansdale/Doylestown line for Center City (2.3-mile area between Delaware River and Schuylkill River from Vine Street to South Street), Philadelphia, on June 4, 2023. (*Brian A. Keates photograph*)

North Wales Station, located in the borough of North Wales, Montgomery County, Pennsylvania, is the location of SEPTA Silverliner V car No. 874, built by Hyundai Rotem, heading a train on the Lansdale/Doylestown Line on May 31, 2019. (*Michael Pearson photograph*)

Reading Railroad No. 901 (1,500-horsepower EMD type FP-7 dual-service passenger and freight-hauling diesel locomotive built in May 1950) is at Norristown, Pennsylvania, powering "The Schuylkill" passenger train on October 22, 1960. SEPTA operated the last regularly scheduled passenger train from Philadelphia to Pottsville, a Budd Rail Diesel Car (RDC), on June 30, 1981. Since June 30, 1981, there has not been any regularly scheduled passenger service to or from Pottsville, Pennsylvania. (*Kenneth C. Springirth photograph*)

On December 30, 2020, SEPTA Silverliner IV car No. 401 is near the Norristown Transportation Center in Norristown, Pennsylvania, for a trip to Philadelphia via the Manayunk/Norristown Line. (*Andrew L. Keates photograph*)

SEPTA Silverliner V car No. 864 built by Hyundai Rotem is at the Wissahickon Station in Northwest Philadelphia on June 10, 2023 for a Manayunk/Norristown Line trip. (*Michael Pearson photograph*)

Leading the way into the Elm Street Station, the last stop on the Manayunk/Norristown Line, in Norristown, Pennsylvania, on June 25, 2023 is SEPTA Silverliner V car No. 877 built by Hyundai Rotem. (*Brian A. Keates photograph*)

SEPTA's 49th Street Station in the Kingsessing neighborhood of Southwest Philadelphia is the location of Silverliner IV car No. 454 on October 20, 2007 with the line known as the Media/Elwyn Line. When service was restored to Wawa on August 21, 2022, it became known as the Media/Wawa Line. Nearby the Chester Avenue bridge carries SEPTA Subway Surface Route 13 trolley over the Media/Wawa Line. (*Kenneth C. Springirth photograph*)

On May 10, 2019, SEPTA Media/Elwyn Line car No. 2405 (one of ten cars [Nos. 2401–2410] built by Bombardier in 1987 for push pull service) is at the Secane Station on the Media/Elwyn Line. (*Michael Pearson photograph*)

SEPTA Silverliner IV car No. 601 is on a wire repair train at the Media repair yard on the Media/Elwyn Line that is used as a crew transport car on March 7, 2020. *(Brian A. Keates photograph)*

On March 7, 2020, Republic locomotive RL1000 No. 61, built in March 1992, is powering the SEPTA wire repair train at the Media repair yard shown in the top picture. This locomotive was used in work train service; however, it was used in commuter service in 1993. Republic Locomotive (located in Greenville, South Carolina) began rebuilding locomotives in 1980, and in 1990 began building new locomotives. *(Brian A. Keates photograph)*

SEPTA Silverliner IV car No. 178 leads a commuter train into the Elwyn Station on January 2, 2021. This was the end of the line before the line opened to Wawa on August 21, 2022. (*Brian A. Keates photograph*)

On March 7, 2020, Silverliner V car No. 725 arrives at Media Station for its run to Philadelphia. (*Brian A. Keates photograph*)

A SEPTA commuter train is in place at the Media yard awaiting departure time headed by Silverliner V car No. 841 on March 7, 2020. (*Brian A. Keates photograph*)

Invited guests have assembled at Wawa, Pennsylvania, for the celebration of the extension of the commuter line from Elwyn to Wawa on August 18, 2022. (*Beth Anne Keates photograph*)

The special advertising wrap on the Silverliner V car No. 863 at the newly opened Wawa Station (in Middletown Township, Delaware County, Pennsylvania) commemorates the opening of the line from Elwyn to Wawa on August 18, 2022. SEPTA announced on July 27, 2022 that Wawa acquired the naming rights for the Wawa Station for $5.4 million for ten years. With restoration of service to Wawa, the Media/Elwyn Line was renamed Media/Wawa Line. (*Beth Anne Keates photograph*)

Silverliner V car No. 864 (with the special Wawa Station advertising wrap on it) with No. 863 behind it (shown in the above photo) are at the Wawa Station on August 18, 2022. (*Beth Anne Keates photograph*)

On August 18, 2022, the special guests are ready for the ribbon-cutting ceremony for the opening of the restored line to Wawa. (*Beth Anne Keates photograph*)

SEPTA Silverliner IV car No. 292 is at the rear of a Philadelphia bound train at the Wawa Station on the Media/Wawa Line on June 14, 2023. (*Brian A. Keates photograph*)

On July 14, 2023, SEPTA Silverliner IV car No. 293 is heading a train out of the Wawa Station for Philadelphia on the Media/Wawa Line. (*Brian A. Keates photograph*)

SEPTA Silverliner V car No. 706 is at the Lansdowne Station in the borough of Lansdowne, Delaware County, Pennsylvania, on its November 27, 2022 trip to Philadelphia on the Media/Wawa Line. Electrified passenger service was inaugurated on the Philadelphia via Lansdowne to West Chester, Pennsylvania, Railroad Line on Sunday December 2, 1928. (*Brian A. Keates photograph*)

Just west of the SEPTA Lansdowne Station behind the Wildman Arms Condominiums, SEPTA Silverliner V car No. 858 is part of a Media/Wawa Line commuter train passing through Lansdowne, Pennsylvania, on January 1, 2023. (*Brian A. Keates photograph*)

On July 1, 2023, Silverliner IV car No. 363 has brought the train to a stop at the Wallingford Station in Nether Providence Township, Delaware County, Pennsylvania, to discharge and pick up passengers on its trip to Philadelphia on the Media/Wawa Line. The station, believed to have been built in 1890, may have been designed by Frank Furness. (*Brian A. Keates photograph*)

SEPTA locomotive No. 906 (type ACS-64 received in April 2018) is powering a train at Wallingford Station on July 17, 2023. The first ACS-64 No. 901 went into service on July 11, 2018. This type of locomotive was designed by Siemens for use in Europe and Asia, and changes were made to comply with United States Standards. (*Michael Pearson photograph*)

On July 1, 2023, Silverliner IV car No. 106 is at the rear of a train at the Wallingford Station heading for Philadelphia. (*Brian A. Keates photograph*)

The Victorian Gothic-style (characterized by brick construction with detailed wood ornamentation) Morton Station in Morton Borough, Delaware County, Pennsylvania, with the handicap ramp in place, is the location on July 13, 2023 of SEPTA Silverliner IV car No. 424 leading a westbound train to Wawa. This station, built in 1867, was rebuilt in 1880 designed by architect Joseph Wilson of the Wilson Brothers & Company architectural firm. (*Beth Anne Keates photograph*)

Looking east at Swarthmore Station in the Borough of Swarthmore in Delaware County, Pennsylvania, SEPTA Silverliner IV car No. 316 is westbound on the Media/Wawa Line on July 13, 2023. The station was originally named Westdale in honor of early settler and painter Benjamin West. It was renamed Swarthmore after Swarthmore College was established in 1864 as a coeducational college by members of the Religious Society of Friends (Quakers). Swarthmore College (located north of SEPTA's Swarthmore Station) has excellent public transit accessibility to the Philadelphia area. (*Beth Anne Keates photograph*)

On July 13, 2023, SEPTA Silverliner IV car No. 382 is on the Media/Wawa Line across the track from the Victorian-style Clifton-Aldan Station in Clifton Heights, a borough in Delaware County, Pennsylvania, on its westbound trip to Wawa, Pennsylvania, near the bridge over the SEPTA Route 102 (69th Street Transportation Center-Sharon Hill) trolley line on Springfield Road. (*Beth Anne Keates photograph*)

Passing the Berwyn Station in the census-designated place of Berwyn in Chester County, Pennsylvania, on SEPTA's Paoli/Thorndale Line is Amtrak locomotive No. 46 (General Electric [GE] type P42DC [Genesis series] built in January 1997 with a maximum speed of 110 miles per hour) eastbound to Philadelphia on May 22, 2022. (*Andrew L. Keates photograph*)

Amtrak locomotive No. 636 (Siemens type ACS-64 built in 2015) is at the rear of a westbound train passing the Berwyn Station on May 15, 2022. ACS-64 locomotives were built at the Siemens factory in Florin, California, near Sacramento, with the first locomotive No. 600 placed in service on February 7, 2014, and the final unit (No. 670) entering revenue service in August 2016. (*Andrew L. Keates photograph*)

On July 1, 2023, Amtrak locomotive No. 663 (Siemens type ACS-64 built in March 2015) is on the rear of a westbound train after stopping at Paoli Station in Paoli, a census-designated place (a closely settled, unincorporated community that is locally recognized, and identified by name) in Chester County, Pennsylvania. This locomotive was designed to be capable of accelerating eighteen Amfleet cars to a maximum speed of 125 miles per hour in a little more than eight minutes. (*Brian A. Keates photograph*)

Amtrak-model Budd Metroliner control car No. 9632 is at the Paoli Station on a westbound run on July 1, 2023. By definition, a control car is a non-powered rail car from which a train can be operated with all of the controls and gauges needed to remotely operate the locomotive. A control car makes it possible to have push-pull operation when located on the end of the train opposite the locomotive, making it possible for the train to reverse direction without having to reverse direction without moving the locomotive or turning the train around. (*Brian A. Keates photograph*)

On July 1, 2023, Silverliner IV car No. 345 is on a westbound train at Paoli Station ready for departure time. A $48 million upgrade station project began in February 2017, which replaced two low-level platforms with a high-level island platform. A pedestrian overpass was constructed over the tracks, plus elevators and ramps were added. A ribbon-cutting ceremony was held marking the completion of this project on September 23, 2019. (*Brian A. Keates photograph*)

SEPTA Silverliner IV car No. 304 is coming into Paoli Station on an eastbound trip to Center City, Philadelphia, on July 1, 2023. (*Brian A. Keates photograph*)

On February 28, 2018, SEPTA Silverliner IV car No. 166 is trailing on an eastbound commuter train at Malvern Station in Malvern, a borough in Chester County, Pennsylvania. This station was originally built by the Pennsylvania Railroad in 1900. (*Andrew L. Keates photograph*)

Westbound SEPTA commuter train headed by SEPTA Silverliner IV commuter car No. 108 is at the Malvern Station on June 19, 2023. (*Michael Pearson photograph*)

SEPTA Siemens ACS-64 locomotive No. 905, built in March 2018, has just pulled a westbound commuter train into the Malvern Station on April 1, 2021. This locomotive is designed with special couplers to keep trains from rolling over, jackknifing, or derailing in a collision. (*Andrew L. Keates photograph*)

On April 1, 2021, SEPTA Silverliner IV car No. 316 brings a westbound passenger train into the Malvern Station. (*Andrew L. Keates photograph*)

Eastbound SEPTA Silverliner IV car No. 404 arrives at the Malvern Station on a cloudy bright August 2, 2017. (*Andrew L. Keates photograph*)

With a light dusting of snow on the ground, on a cloudy, yet bright January 17, 2018, SEPTA Silverliner IV car No. 385 rolls into the Exton Station in Exton, which is a census-designated place in West Whiteland Township in Chester County, Pennsylvania. (*Andrew L. Keates photograph*)

On a wintery January 17, 2018, Silverliner V car No. 852 is at the end of an eastbound commuter train at Exton ready for departure time. Improvements were completed at the Exton Station on March 2, 2020 as follows: high-level platforms were constructed for fully accessible boarding, a new station building was constructed with restrooms for customers, and LED platform lighting was installed. (*Andrew L. Keates photograph*)

Westbound SEPTA locomotive No. 908 (Siemens type ACS-64 built in April 2018) is at Exton Station on June 19, 2023. Siemens has noted that the locomotive allows for self-diagnosis of technical issues by "The on-board computer system can notify the engineer and operator of any maintenance issues and can take self-corrective action to maintain operation of the locomotive and ensure safety." (*Michael Pearson photograph*)

Amtrak locomotive No. 612 (Siemens type ACS-64 built in 2014) is westbound rolling past Exton Station on March 23, 2017. The design of this locomotive was based on the EuroSprinter group of electric locomotives built for the European market by Siemens with the first prototype built in 1992 for the Deutsche Bahn AG (national railway company of Germany controlled by the German government). (*Andrew L. Keates photograph*)

SEPTA No. 2302 type AEM-7 locomotive, built in November 1987, is pulling into the snow-covered Exton Station on March 16, 2017. After Amtrak took over United States passenger service on May 1, 1971, there was a need to replace the reliable but aging GG-1 locomotives. After testing various models, the Rc4 locomotive built by the General Swedish Electric Company (Allmanna Svenska Elektriska Aktiebolaget [ASEA]) was chosen and became the design of the AEM-7 electric locomotive (twin-cab four-axle 7,000-horsepower built by Electro-Motive Division of General Motors Corporation [EMD] and ASEA). (*Brian A. Keates photograph*)

On February 24, 2018, SEPTA's 51.15-foot-long type AEM-7 electric locomotive No. 2306, built in December 1987, is approaching the Exton Station powering a westbound commuter train. This type of locomotive has been affectionately known as a "toaster" due to its compact, boxy design. (*Andrew L. Keates photograph*)

Westbound SEPTA Silverliner V car No. 818 leads a westbound train into Exton Station on May 3, 2017. (*Brian A. Keates photograph*)

On October 20, 2017, Norfolk Southern Railway (NS) locomotive No. 6707 (EMD type SD60 six-axle 3,800-horsepower diesel electric originally built in August 1989 as No. 6852 for Consolidated Rail Corporation [Conrail]) is powering a short local train on SEPTA's Paoli/Thorndale line near Whitford Station where NS has permission to use SEPTA's tracks. (*Andrew L. Keates photograph*)

Amtrak locomotive No. 145 (GE type P42DC built in February 2001 and painted in the Phase III paint scheme with the red, white, and blue stripes of equal width) is leading an eastbound passenger train past Whitford Station in Exton, Chester County, Pennsylvania, on January 31, 2021. This picture shows the abandoned railway bridge that is directly above the station site that was built in 1906 by the Pennsylvania Railroad crossing (or flying) over it. With the decline in freight traffic in the 1970s, Consolidated Rail Corporation (Conrail) abandoned the freight line in 1989. (*Andrew L. Keates photograph*)

On November 8, 2021, Amtrak locomotive No. 669 (Siemens ACS-64 built in 2016) leads a westbound passenger train past Whitford Station. According to the Siemens' information sheet, this locomotive has "crash energy managements like front-end strength and a crumple zone for collision with large objects." (*Andrew L. Keates photograph*)

Amtrak locomotive No. 662 (Siemens ACS-64 built in 2015) is passing past Whitford Station on January 19, 2022. According to Siemens' literature, "The electro-dynamic brake system of the ACS-64 has the ability to put a maximum of 5MW of electricity back into the catenary during regenerative breaking. The regenerative braking can feed up to 100 percent of the energy generated during braking back to the power grid." (*Andrew L. Keates photograph*)

On November 8, 2021, Amtrak locomotive No. 108 (GE type P42DC built in August 1997 and painted commemorating Amtrak's fiftieth anniversary) is pulling an eastbound passenger train past Whitford Station. (*Andrew L. Keates photograph*)

An Amtrak maintenance of way train is waiting for the next assignment at Whitford Station on February 1, 2022 powered by locomotive No. 527 (EMD type GP38H-3 [formerly General Motors Diesel GP40TC built for GO Transit which serves the Greater Horseshoe region of Ontario, Canada with its hub at Union Station in Toronto]). There were eight of these GP40TC locomotives, manufactured between 1966 and 1968, sold to Amtrak, modifications made for Amtrak, redesignated GP40H, and numbered 520–527. In 2005, Norfolk Southern Railway rebuilt these locomotives at their Juniata Shops in Altoona, Pennsylvania, as type GP38H-3 and retained Nos. 520–527. (*Andrew L. Keates photograph*)

On March 9, 2021 Amtrak locomotive No. 527 (shown in above photo) is facing westbound, while SEPTA Siemens ACS-64 locomotive No. 902, built in 2018, is leading an eastbound train near the Downingtown Station, in the borough of Downingtown, Pennsylvania. (*Andrew L. Keates photograph*)

On June 19, 2023, SEPTA locomotive No. 908 (Siemens ACS64 built in 2018) is making a station stop at Whitford Station. (*Michael Pearson photograph*)

SEPTA Silverliner V No. 722 is on the rear of an eastbound train at Thorndale Station in Thorndale, a census-designated place in Chester County, Pennsylvania, on July 1, 2023 waiting for departure time. According to the SEPTA Paoli/Thorndale Line August 27, 2023 schedule, service from Thorndale, Downingtown, Whitford, and Exton only operates Monday to Saturday. (*Brian A. Keates photograph*)

On July 1, 2023, Amtrak locomotive No. 634 (Siemens type ACS-64 delivered in 2015) is eastbound at the SEPTA Thorndale Station. Structural changes were made to the ACS-64 design to comply with American crashworthiness requirements including anti-climbing features and structural strengthening of the cab. (*Brian A. Keates photograph*)

Amtrak catenary maintenance vehicle No. A 15515 is at the Thorndale Station waiting for its next assignment. The vehicle is self-propelled by a diesel engine to allow for the vehicle to operate when the power is shut off to the overhead wires for worker safety or if there is a power failure. While catenary maintenance normally involves planned inspections and repairs, this vehicle can also be used to clear ice and icicles from the wires plus bridge and tunnel inspection. (*Brian A. Keates photograph*)

North Philadelphia Station, located on North Broad Street in the North Philadelphia neighborhood of Philadelphia, Pennsylvania, on July 2, 2021 (used by SEPTA's Chestnut Hill West Line and Trenton Line in April 2023) is the location of an Amtrak Acela Express train set powered by locomotive No. 2016 (one of forty power cars [Nos. 2000–2039]). Bombardier Alstrom was selected on March 15, 1996 to build twenty train sets each consisting of two power cars and six coaches. An Acela inaugural run was made on November 16, 2000 led by power car No. 2020 with No. 2009 at the rear. Revenue service began on December 11, 2000. (*Andrew L. Keates photograph*)

On July 22, 2021, Amtrak locomotive No. 602 (Siemens type ACS-64 built in 2014) is powering a train at North Philadelphia Station. (*Andrew L. Keates photograph*)

Southbound Amtrak locomotive No. 46 (type P42DC built by GE in January 1997) is passing the North Philadelphia Station platform on July 22, 2021. This type of locomotive has a monocoque (French for single shell) carbody design in which loads are supported by the object's external skin like an eggshell. This station opened in the 1870s as the New York Junction and Germantown. A new Beaux Arts-style station was completed in 1901. Between 1912 and 1915, it was enlarged and was renamed North Philadelphia Station. In 1991, Amtrak constructed a smaller station. The original station building was renovated in 1999 for commercial space. The 1901-built station building was listed on the National Register of Historic Places on July 8, 1999. (*Andrew L. Keates photograph*)

On July 22, 2021, Amtrak locomotive No. 605 (Siemens type ACS-64 built in 2014) is leading a train at North Philadelphia Station. (*Andrew L. Keates photograph*)

SEPTA Silverliner IV No. 442 is at the Torresdale Station in the Torresdale neighborhood of Northeast Philadelphia heading for Trenton, New Jersey, on the Trenton Line on April 29, 2013. This station is on the Northeast Corridor owned by Amtrak; however, Amtrak does not stop at this station. (*Kenneth C. Springirth photograph*)

Shown at North Philadelphia Station on July 22, 2021 heading to Philadelphia from New York City is Amtrak Beech Grove car No. 10001, built for Amtrak by the Budd Corporation in 1977 as a standard eighty-four-seat Amfleet coach No. 21222. It was damaged in an accident in 1978 and withdrawn from service. It was rebuilt at Amtrak's Beech Grove shops in 1984 as No. 10001, renamed Beech Grove, and is used as a business/inspection car with three bedrooms, dining room, kitchen, observation room, and exterior headlights. (*Andrew L. Keates photograph*)

Frankford Junction near the intersection of Frankford Avenue and Butler St. in Philadelphia, Pennsylvania, on the Trenton Line on February 8, 1978 is the location of the first GG1 No. 4800 (frame, running gear, and [only one] with riveted body built by Baldwin locomotive Works and completed in 1934 at General Electric in Erie, Pennsylvania, with installation of electrical components) shown in Conrail blue. On January 28, 1935, No. 4800 inaugurated electric passenger service between Philadelphia and, Washington D.C., and was retired by Conrail in October 1979. It was placed on display at the Railroad Museum of Pennsylvania at Strasburg on November 20, 1982. (*Photographer Alfred Gaus Used with permission from Audio Visual Designs [www.audiovisualdesigns.com]*)

On May 31, 1964, Pennsylvania Railroad (PRR) GG1 No. 4922 (built with General Electric gear in August 1942 at PRR's Altoona Works and later scrapped) and No. 4853 (built with Westinghouse electrical gear in June 1935 at PRR's Altoona Works and later scrapped) are near Girard Avenue in Philadelphia. (*Kenneth C. Springirth photograph*)

SEPTA locomotive No. 52 (EMD type SW1200 four-axle diesel switcher originally built in November 1954 as No. 2034 for the Chicago, Milwaukee, St. Paul & Pacific Railroad [Milwaukee Road] and renumbered 639) is taking a number of AEM-7 locomotives and one ALP-44M locomotive to the scrapyard past the Levittown Train Station on the SEPTA Trenton Line on May 14, 2022. (*Andrew L. Keates photograph*)

On May 14, 2022, SEPTA No. 2308 (Asea Brown Boveri [ABB] type ALP-44M [micropressor] electric locomotive built in October 1996 that was part of a damage settlement resulting from the late delivery of N5 cars for the Norristown High Speed Line) and SEPTA No. 2302 (EMD & ASEA type AEM-7 electric locomotive built in November 1987) are some of the locomotives in the above picture passing the Levittown Train Station heading for the Morristown scrapyard via the SEPTA Trenton Line and were scrapped before the end of 2022. (*Andrew L. Keates photograph*)

SEPTA No. 2304 (AEM7 built by EMD in December 1987) brings up the rear of a train of AEM-7 electric locomotives plus one ALP-44M electric locomotive that have been sold for scrap passing the Levittown, Pennsylvania, train station on May 14, 2022 (shown on the page 56 top and bottom pictures). The Pennsylvania Railroad's original Tullytown Station was replaced by the Levittown-Tullytown Station on April 26, 1953. SEPTA later changed the station name to Levittown. (*Andrew L. Keates photograph*)

On May 14, 2022, SEPTA Silverliner V lead train car No. 837 comes to a stop at the Levittown Station on its run to Center City, Philadelphia. This station received a $37.3 million reconstruction project which included high-level platforms, a pedestrian overpass, and parking improvements which were completed in October 2019. (*Andrew L. Keates photograph*)

SEPTA Silverliner V car No. 717 is waiting for permission to pull into the Trenton Transit Center in Trenton, New Jersey, on June 19, 2023. Trenton is the only city in New Jersey that serves the three major railway systems in the state: Amtrak, NJ Transit, and SEPTA. In addition, across the street from the Trenton Transit Center is the northern terminus of the River Line, a light rail line that has some features of a commuter rail line connecting Trenton with Camden, New Jersey. (*Beth Anne Keates photograph*)

Holmesburg Junction Station on the Trenton Line is the location of SEPTA Silverliner V car No. 701 on June 3, 2023. At Holmesburg Junction, the Bustleton Branch splits from the mainline tracks and serves Northeast Philadelphia. Pennsylvania Railroad passenger service on the 4.1-mile section between Holmesburg Junction and Bustleton ended on February 13, 1926 because of a ridership decline; however, freight service is operated by the East Penn Railroad on this line which is now known as their North East Philadelphia Line. (*Michael Pearson photograph*)

On June 3, 2023, SEPTA Silverliner IV car No. 429 is at the Holmesburg Junction Station on its Trenton Line trip to Center City, Philadelphia. This station is in the Holmesburg neighborhood of Northeast Philadelphia. (*Michael Pearson photograph*)

SEPTA diesel switcher No. 80 is on the rear of a New Hope & Ivyland steam excursion train serving as an escort on the SEPTA Warminster Line on May 18, 2019. This locomotive was originally Atchison Topeke & Santa Fe No. 2861 (EMD four-axle 1,500-horsepower diesel electric type GP7 built in June 1953) that was rebuilt to type GP7u with a low, short hood and renumbered 2075 in July 1974. It was retired in 1992 and sold to Santa Fe Southern Railway and became No. 92. It was rebuilt by Knoxville Locomotive Works in Louisville, Kentucky, and became No. 80. (*Andrew L. Keates photograph*)

New Hope and Ivyland Railroad steam locomotive No. 40 (2-8-0 wheel arrangement "Consolidation" type with two leading wheels on one axle, eight powered and coupled driving wheels on four axles, and no trailing wheels) is powering a steam excursion passing the SEPTA Gwynedd Valley Station in Lower Gwynedd Township, Montgomery County, Pennsylvania, via SEPTA's Lansdale/Doylestown Line on May 18, 2019. *(Andrew L. Keates photograph)*

This May 18, 2019 view of the New Hope & Ivyland Steam special with locomotive No. 40 near the SEPTA Gwynedd Valley Station showing a 1947 Plymouth special deluxe automobile. The locomotive was built by the Baldwin Locomotive Works in Philadelphia, Pennsylvania, on December 2, 1925 for the Lancaster & Chester Railroad in Lancaster, South Carolina. In 1947, it was sold to the Cliffside Railroad in North Carolina and was retired from service in 1962. From 1981 to retirement in 1986, No. 40 was the New Hope Railroad's main steam-powered locomotive. Excursions were operated with No. 40 on May 18, 2019 from Gwynedd Valley Station to North Wales, Pennsylvania, to celebrate the 150th anniversary of North Wales, which was incorporated in 1869. *(Andrew L. Keates photograph)*

On September 26, 2016, SEPTA Silverliner IV car No. 139 is near the SEPTA Warminster Station in Warminster Township, Bucks County, Pennsylvania. (*Kenneth C. Springirth photograph*)

SEPTA locomotive No. 910 (type ACS 64 [Siemens] built in 2018) is at the SEPTA Warminster Station waiting for departure time as train No. 4571 on April 2, 2019. The Warminster Line January 8, 2023 schedule shows that same train number departing Warminster at 5:21 p.m. Monday through Friday running local to Jenkintown-Wyncote, express to Temple University, arriving there at 6:09 p.m. and continuing as a local Paoli/Thorndale train, making every stop arriving 7:42 p.m. at Thorndale. (*Michael Pearson photograph*)

On September 26, 2016, SEPTA Silverliner IV car No. 432 is making a passenger stop at the Glenside Station located in Glenside, a census-designated place in Montgomery County, Pennsylvania, on SEPTA's West Trenton Line. It opened as Tacony Station in 1855, later renamed Abington Station, and in 1888 became Glenside Station. The station is served by the Lansdale/Doylestown and Warminster Lines. (*Kenneth C. Springirth* photograph)

SEPTA Silverliner IV car No. 424 is heading a westbound commuter train at Woodbourne Station in Middletown Township in Bucks County, Pennsylvania, on December 11, 2022. The CSX Transportation Railroad Trenton Subdivision parallels SEPTA's West Trenton Line from Neshaminy Falls, Pennsylvania, to Ewing, New Jersey. (*Brian A. Keates photograph*)

On July 25, 2021, a westbound SEPTA Silverliner commuter train at Woodbourne Station on the West Trenton Line is passed by an eastbound CSX freight train, on a parallel track, powered by GE-built locomotive No. 3379 (type ET44AH 4,400-horsepower [like an ES44AC but designated ES44AH by CSX because it is heavy-ballasted] one of 100 locomotives [Nos. 3375–3474] of this type built during 2016–2017). There were 125 type ET44 AH locomotives (Nos. 3250–3374) built for CSX in 2015. (*Brian A. Keates photograph*)

A westbound CSX freight train headed by locomotive No. 5431 (GE type ES44DC built in February 2007 [one of 302 locomotives, Nos. 5200–5501, downgraded to ES40DC 4,000-horsepower by CSX by 2010]) is passing Woodbourne Station on July 25, 2021. (*Brian A. Keates photograph*)

On December 11, 2022, an eastbound SEPTA train headed by Silverliner IV car No. 401 is rolling past the Woodbourne Station located on Woodbourne Road in Middletown Township, Pennsylvania, on the SEPTA West Trenton Line. (*Brian A. Keates photograph*)

SEPTA Silverliner V car No. 722 is making a stop at the Woodbourne Station on its westbound trip to Center City, Philadelphia, on December 11, 2022. (*Brian A. Keates photograph*)

On June 17, 2023, SEPTA Silver IV car No. 142, leading a westbound train, has made a stop at the Woodbourne Station. During November 2002, new station facilities were constructed at this site. Due to the configuration of this three-track area (two passenger tracks and one CSX freight track), paved areas were constructed to reach the center passenger track. (*Brian A. Keates photograph*)

SEPTA Silverliner car No. 169 is at Woodbourne Station bringing up the rear on a westbound train out of West Trenton, New Jersey, on June 17, 2023. (*Brian A. Keates photograph*)

SEPTA West Trenton Line train No. 3545 headed by Silverliner IV car No. 285, according to the April 16, 2023 schedule, is at the Yardley Station in the borough of Yardley in Bucks County, Pennsylvania, at 5:53 p.m. for its trip to Center City, Philadelphia, and through routed on the Paoli/Thorndale Line arriving 7:45 p.m. at Malvern. The North Pennsylvania Railroad plus Delaware & Bound Brook Railroad opened a line from Jenkintown, Pennsylvania, to Bound Brook, New Jersey, on May 1, 1876 which was leased by the Philadelphia & Reading Railroad on May 14, 1879. Electrified Philadelphia to West Trenton, New Jersey, service was opened by the Reading Railroad on July 26, 1931. (*Michael Pearson photograph*)

SEPTA Silverliner IV car No. 450 is bringing up the rear of an eastbound train coming into a mini yard at West Trenton, New Jersey, on June 17, 2023. (*Brian A. Keates photograph*)

Pulling up for a stop at the SEPTA West Trenton, New Jersey, Station (northern terminus of SEPTA's West Trenton Line) on June 17, 2023 is eastbound Silverliner IV car No. 399. (*Brian A. Keates photograph*)

On June 17, 2023, SEPTA Silverliner IV car No. 399 pulls an eastbound train into the West Trenton, New Jersey, train station. Originally built in 1929 by the Reading Railroad, the station's Georgian Revival style features brick construction with a hipped slate roof and symmetrical placement of windows. On June 22, 1984, it was listed on the National Register of Historic Places. (*Brian A. Keates photograph*)

On a snowy February 2, 2021, SEPTA Silverliner V car No. 725 is at the Highland Avenue Station in Chester, Delaware County, Pennsylvania, on SEPTA's Wilmington/Newark Line. Amtrak trains do not stop at this station. (*Andrew L. Keates photograph*)

On July 17, 2023, the Chester Transportation Center in the city of Chester, Delaware County, Pennsylvania, is the location of a SEPTA Wilmington/Newark Line train powered by locomotive No. 913, type ACS64 (Siemens) built in 2018. (*Michael Pearson photograph*)

SEPTA Silverliner V car No. 709 is arriving at the Wilmington Station in the city of Wilmington, New Castle County, Delaware, on July 19, 2023 via the SEPTA Wilmington/Newark Line. Designed by architect Frank Furness, this station, with its Romanesque architectural style that provides an impression of solidity and strength, was completed on June 29, 1908. It was added to the National Register of Historic Places on July 6, 1976. (*Beth Anne Keates photograph*)

Silverliner V car No. 709 is awaiting departure time from the Wilmington, Delaware, Station on July 19, 2023. In addition to SEPTA Regional Rail Service, this station is a major Amtrak station. (*Beth Anne Keates photograph*)

On July 10, 2023, SEPTA Silverliner IV four-car commuter train headed by car No. 128 is at the Newark Station located in the city of Newark, New Castle County, Delaware, on the Wilmington/Newark Line. SEPTA service was extended to Newark in 1997. The Newark Station is the southern terminus of SEPTA's Wilmington/Newark Line. (*Michael Pearson photograph*)

SEPTA Silverliner V car No. 859 is in the lineup of cars being cleaned at the station in Newark, Delaware, on July 19, 2023. (*Beth Anne Keates photograph*)

2

Philadelphia Trolley History

On January 21, 1858, the first horse-drawn street railway was introduced by the Philadelphia & Delaware Railroad on 5th and 6th Street from Kensington to Southwark. The first electric streetcar was introduced by the Catherine & Bainbridge Street Passenger Railway Company on December 15, 1892. Electric trolley cars were so successful that within five years, on January 15, 1897, the Callowhill Street line ended horse car operation in Philadelphia.

The Philadelphia Transportation Company (PTC) was established on January 1, 1940 by the merger of the Philadelphia Rapid Transit Company (PRT) and some small independent transit companies in and around Philadelphia. During 1940, it ordered 130 Presidents Conference Committee (PCC) trolley cars, fifty trackless trolleys, and fifty-three buses. The number of trolley cars in service declined from 1,612 in 1953 to 557 in 1958. In 1953, trolley car service ended on Route 18 (South 22nd and 23rd Streets) and 65 (York Road–6th and 7th Streets). National City Lines acquired PTC in 1955, and trolley car service ended in 1955 on Routes 5 (Frankford–2nd and 3rd Streets), 7 (Strawberry Mansion–22nd and 23rd Streets), 33 (North 22nd Street), 37 (Westinghouse–Subway), 38 (Baring Street–Subway), 54 (Lehigh Avenue), 57 (Jefferson and Master Streets), 63 (Catherine and Bainbridge Streets), 66 Holmesburg (Frankford Avenue), 70 (52nd Street–Bala), and 81 (Passyunk Avenue). In 1956, trolley car service ended on Route 2 (15th and 16th Streets), 3 (Frankford–Columbia Avenue), 8 (Dauphin and Susquehanna Avenue), 9 (Strawberry Mansion–4th and 5th Streets), 12 (Grays Ferry), 21 (North 17th and 18 Streets), 26 (Olney Avenue), 31 (Market and 63rd Streets), 39 (Dauphin and Susquehanna Avenue), 40 (Lombard and South Streets), 42 (West Spruce Street), 43 (Spring Garden Street), 48 (Fairmount–Arch Street), 52 (Chelten Mid-vale), 64 (Federal and Wharton Streets), and 79 (Snyder Avenue). In 1957, trolley car service ended on Route 17 (South 19th and 20th Streets), 20 (12th and 13th Streets), 32 (South 17th and 18th Street), 41 (63rd Street), and 46 (58th and 60th Street). In 1958, trolley car service was cut back on Route 6 from Glenside to City Line). From 1953 to 1958, PTC abandoned thirty-five trolley car lines, and the number of trolley cars declined from 1,612 in 1953 to 557 in 1958 serving the thirteen surviving trolley car routes: 6 (City Line to Ogontz), 10, 11, 13, 15, 23, 34, 36, 47 (southern portion was converted to bus operation on July 9, 1967), 50, 53, 60, and 62.

On September 30, 1968, the Southeastern Pennsylvania Transportation Authority (SEPTA) acquired PTC. Under SEPTA, the following trolley car routes were converted to bus operation: Route 47 (remaining northern half) June 15, 1969, Route 6 (City Line to Ogontz) June 11, 1986, Route 23 February 27, 1992, Route 50 October 11, 1980, Route 53 temporarily June 1981 and permanent May 16, 1985, Route 56 June 12, 1992, Route 60 September 4, 1977, and Route 62 in 1971 became a rush-hour extension of Route 13. It should be noted that Route 15 was converted to bus operation in 1992, restored to trolley car operation using PCC cars that had been rebuilt into PCC II cars by Brookville Equipment Corporation on September 5, 2005, and returned temporarily to bus operation on January 21, 2020 for a rebuilding of the PCC II cars. As of June 16, 2024, eight restored PCC cars were placed in service on Route 15 with buses still being used until restoration of the ten remaining PCC cars is completed. As of November 3, 2023, SEPTA operates five city subway surface trolley car Routes 10, 11, 13, 34, and 36. The SEPTA suburban system operates 2 routes Media and Sharon Hill plus the Norristown High Speed Line. On February 23, 2023, SEPTA awarded a $714,239,455 contract to Alstrom Transportation Inc. to build 130 trolleys with delivery scheduled to begin in 2027 and completed by the end of 2030.

Route 6 Ogontz Avenue Line

Route 6 opened as the Glenside Line in 1924 operating between the Willow Grove Depot with City Line and Ogontz Avenue via Limekiln Pike. The line was extended to Broad Street and Olney Avenue in 1929. On June 20, 1948, Presidents Conference Committee (PCC) trolley cars went into service on Route 6. This once-popular trolley car line to the Willow Grove Amusement Park was replaced by buses on the section north of Cheltenham Avenue to the Willow Grove Park on June 8, 1958. The remaining 2.9-mile Route 6 section operated from Broad and Olney Avenue to Ogontz and Cheltenham Avenues at the City Line and was converted by SEPTA to bus operation on January 12, 1986.

Route 10 Lancaster Avenue Line

The Southeastern Pennsylvania Transportation Authority (SEPTA) 5.8-mile Route 10 began before 1887 operating between Belmont and Jefferson and Front and Walnut. In 1902, the Philadelphia Rapid Transit Company was formed and began constructing electric trolley car lines in Philadelphia. On December 15, 1906, the line became part of the subway-surface trolley system by the Philadelphia Rapid Transit Company. In 1926, the line was extended to 63rd and Malvern Avenue.

Route 11 Woodland Avenue Line

The SEPTA 7-mile Route 11 began on July 2, 1858 when the West Philadelphia Passenger Railway opened for business after completing laying tracks from 3rd Street on Market Street to 41st Street in West

Philadelphia. In 1858, the Philadelphia & Darby Railroad Company began transporting passengers via Darby Road (Woodland Avenue today). On December 15, 1906, the line was included into the subway-surface trolley car system by the Philadelphia Rapid Transit Company. The line has an at-grade crossing on Main Street at 6th Street in Darby with the Baltimore & Ohio Railroad, which later became the CSX Transportation Railroad, an active freight rail line.

Route 13 Chester Avenue Line

The SEPTA 6.3-mile Route 13 started in 1907 as an extension of the Chestnut Street Line and operated between 9th and Main in Darby to 65th and Kingsessing. The two lines were combined into one line operating between 9th and Main in Darby to Front and Chestnut in Philadelphia. On September 9, 1956, the line was rerouted into the subway-surface tunnel with its terminus at Juniper and Market Streets. The February 26, 2023 schedule shows regular service from 13th and Market in Philadelphia to Chester and Callahan Avenues in Yeadon with certain trips extended to the Darby Transportation Center

Route 15 Girard Avenue Line

The SEPTA 8.4-mile Route 15 opened as the Richmond & Schuylkill River Passenger Railway from 2nd Street to 31st Street in July 1859. It reorganized as the Fairmount Park & Delaware River Passenger Railway on June 14, 1864 and was merged onto the Germantown Passenger Railway on February 15, 1866. The People's Passenger Railway leased the line on October 1, 1881. On July 1, 1896, the Union Traction Company leased the People's Passenger Railway. The line was extended west to 60th Street in 1900 and further west to 63rd Street and Girard Avenue plus east to Richmond Street and Allegheny Avenue in 1903. It later replaced the Bridesburg Line to Bridesburg. Route 15 was cut back to Richmond and Westmoreland on February 24,1956. SEPTA replaced trolley cars with buses on September 13, 1992. With the exception of a brief period when Kawasaki cars from Route 10 (made surplus during a water main replacement on a portion of Route 10) were used on Route 15, trolley cars did not return to Route 15 until September 4, 2005. During that time period, SEPTA rehabilitated the tracks, repaired the overhead wires, and had Brookville Equipment Corporation completely rebuild eighteen PCC cars, including installing air conditioning and wheelchair lift for Americans with Disabilities compliance (ADA). On January 21, 2020, buses replaced the trolley cars because of a reconstruction project for Interstate 95 and a need to rehabilitate rusted trolley car bodies. On June 16, 2024, SEPTA placed eight restored PCC trolleys back in service on Route 15. Buses will continue to be used on Route 15 until the ten remaining PCC trolleys are completely rebuilt.

Route 23 Germantown Avenue Line

The SEPTA 12.8-mile Route 23 opened before 1877 operating from Germantown Depot to 8th and Dauphin Streets. The line was merged with the 4th and 8th Street trolleys and became the Pelham Line. In 1913, the line, combined with the Mermaid and Chestnut Hill Line in 1913, became the Germantown–10th and 11th Streets Line. In 1920, the northern terminus was extended to the Bethlehem Pike Loop. The southern terminus was extended to 11th Street and Pattison Avenue in 1926, and south to 10th Street and Bigler Avenue in 1957. During 1947 and 1948, the vintage "Nearside" cars were replaced by PCC cars. On December 29, 1957, Route 20 (operating on 12th and 13th Streets) was eliminated and combined with Route 23. Route 23 trolley cars were moved from Germantown Depot to Luzerne Depot which became the depot housing the six remaining North Philadelphia trolley car routes: 6, 23, 50, 53, 56, and 60. Buses permanently replaced Route 23 trolley cars, the second longest trolley car line in North America on February 27, 1992. At that time, Route 501 Queen in Toronto, Canada, was the longest trolley car line (15 miles long) in North America. As of October 2023, the 42-mile Coast tram in Belgium from De Penne near the French border to Knokke-Heist near the Dutch border is the world's longest tram line.

Route 34 Baltimore Avenue Line

The SEPTA 5.5-mile Route 34, once known as the Angora Line, was routed into the subway-surface system on December 15, 1906. In 1912, the western terminus became Baltimore Avenue and 61st Street in Angora, a neighborhood in southwestern Philadelphia where it connected with the Delaware County & Philadelphia Electric Railway which operated trolley service to Media, Pennsylvania. During the COVID-19 Pandemic, Route 34 ceased operation in April 2020, and service resumed on May 17, 2020.

Route 36 Elmwood Avenue Line

The SEPTA 7.2-mile Route 36 started as the Elmwood Avenue Line in 1904 by the Philadelphia Rapid Transit Company operating between Island Road and Elmwood Avenue and Paschall and Grays Ferry Avenue. In 1905, service was extended to 9th and Arch Streets via Spruce and Pine. On November 5, 1955, Route 36 was rerouted into the subway-surface tunnel and extended to the Westinghouse Plant in Essington replacing Route 37 trolley car service. The twenty-four-hour "Owl" service was transferred from Route 37 to Route 36 at the same time. Service at the western terminus was cut back to 94th and Eastwick Avenue on September 9, 1956. Service was cut back again to 88th and Eastwick Avenue on August 15, 1962. Service was cut back again to 84th Street on January 5, 1966; however, it was extended back to 88th Street and Eastwick Avenue on December 11, 1972. Service was cut back to 80th Street and Eastwick on April 26, 1975.

Route 47 Godfrey 8th and 9th Streets Line

The SEPTA 8.9-mile Route 47 opened from Front and Arch to 15th and Glenwood on July 6, 1910. On November 4, 1951, it operated from 5th and Godfrey to 8th and Wolf. Construction of the Port Authority Transit Corporation (PATCO) line under 8th Street in Philadelphia resulted in the Philadelphia Transportation Company (PTC) converting the southern portion of the line to bus operation on July 9, 1967. Under the Southeastern Pennsylvania

Transportation Authority (SEPTA), the northern portion of Route 47 was converted to bus operation on June 15, 1969.

Route 50 Lawndale 4th and 5th Streets

The SEPTA 11.3-mile Route 50 opened on April 13, 1913 from 5th and Jackson to Fox Chase. The line was cut back to Lawndale Loop on January 27, 1956 with the southern terminus at either 4th and Ritner or 6th and Oregon Avenue. Rush-hour service to Lawndale Loop ended October 7, 1968; however, it was restored on October 16, 1972. The line was converted to bus operation on October 12, 1980.

Route 53 Wayne Avenue-Erie Avenue

The SEPTA 4.6-mile Route 53 opened from Wayne and Carpenter to 13th and Locust on April 15, 1904. On September 7, 1930, the line operated from 10th and Luzerne to Wayne and Carpenter. Route 53 was the first Philadelphia trolley line to receive Presidents' Conference Committee trolley cars. On Sundays, trolley car Routes 53 and 75 operated as one route which ended when Route 75 was converted to trackless trolley operation in 1948. Route 53 was converted to bus operation on May 16, 1985.

Route 56 Erie Avenue-Torresdale Avenue

The SEPTA 7.6-mile Route 56, established in 1907, originally operated between 2nd and Tioga and Pulaski and Hunting Park Avenue with the western terminal established at 23rd and Venango in 1926. It operated from Torresdale-Cottman Loop to 23rd and Venango Loop on September 2, 1928 and was converted to bus operation on June 14, 1992.

Route 60 Allegheny Avenue

The SEPTA 5.3-mile Route 60 opened from Richmond-Allegheny to 17th Allegheny on November 1, 1906. On September 10, 1939, it operated from Richmand-Allegheny to Ridge-Allegheny. On May 16, 1956, it operated from Richmond-Westmoreland Loop to 35th-Allegheny Loop. Buses replaced Route 60 trolley cars on September 4, 1977.

Route 62 Darby-Yeadon

The SEPTA, less than a mile long, Route 62 was originally built as an extension of the Philadelphia Rapid Transit Chester Avenue trolley line and opened to Darby on June 1, 1907. The other end of the Chester Avenue line was at Front and Chestnut Streets in Philadelphia. Route 13 was cut back to Mt. Moriah Cemetery, and the Route 62 shuttle line was created to run from Mt. Moriah to 9th and Main Streets in Darby. On June 19, 1927, a new loop was completed on the Route 13 line at Chester Avenue and Callahan in Yeadon. The Route 62 trolley was shortened to run only from Yeadon to Darby. On January 24, 1971, Route 13 was extended daily to Darby for certain rush hour and weekend trips. Route 62 was then discontinued.

Ogontz Avenue at Medary Avenue in the Ogontz/Belfield neighborhood in the upper northern part of Philadelphia is the location of Philadelphia Transportation Company (PTC) Route 6 Presidents' Conference Committee (PCC) car No. 2126. This car, delivered in September 1948 and powered by four Westinghouse type 1432J motors, was one of fifty cars (Nos. 2091–2140) ordered from St. Louis Car Company in July 1946. The car received a general overhaul in January 1982 and was sold to the Municipal Railway of San Francisco for parts in October 1992. *(Kenneth C. Springirth photograph)*

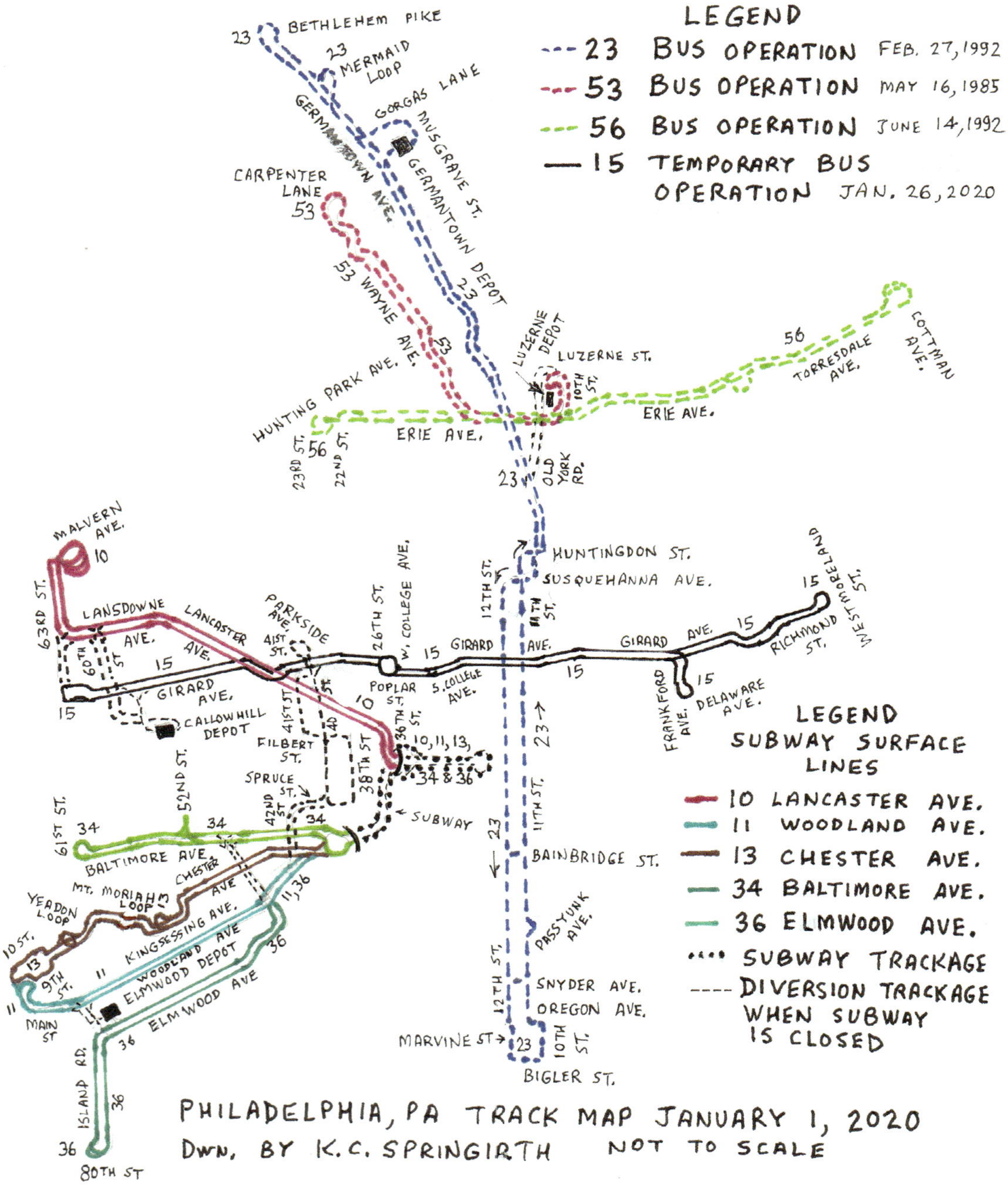

This map shows restoration of Route 15 (Girard Avenue Line) trolley service effective June 16, 2024 with eight restored trolleys in service and until the remaining ten trolleys are completed buses will be used to achieve the needed service frequency.

On Olney Avenue crossing Broad Street in the Olney neighborhood of North Philadelphia finds Philadelphia Transportation Company (PTC) Route 6 PCC car No. 2534 carefully passing through this busy intersection on May 31, 1968. This car, delivered in December 1940 (one of eighty electric/air cars [Nos. 2501–2580] built by St. Louis Car Company equipped with General Electric type 1198F3 motors) was scrapped in March 1982. (*Kenneth C. Springirth photograph*)

On January 11, 1986, SEPTA Route 6 PCC car No. 2716 is at the Route 6 City Line loop waiting for departure time. Built by St. Louis Car Company, this "all electric" car was delivered in March 1947. It was one of twenty-five cars (Nos. 2701–2725), each equipped with four Westinghouse type 1432 motors. This car received a general overhaul in November 1981 and was later sold to Brookville Equipment Corporation. (*Kenneth C. Springirth photograph*)

A sunny January 11, 1986 finds SEPTA "all electric" PCC car No. 2168 at the Route 6 City Line Loop. Powered by four General Electric type 1220A motors, this car was delivered in July 1948. It was one of sixty cars (Nos. 2141–2200) built by St. Louis Car Company and received June–August 1948. During 1992–1996, this was the "Chestnut Hill Trolley." It was sold to the Baltimore Streetcar Museum in 2009. (*Kenneth C. Springirth photograph*)

On May 31, 1969, SEPTA Route 10 PCC car No. 2100 (delivered in August 1948) is on Lansdowne Avenue ready to cross 60th Street in the Carroll Park neighborhood of West Philadelphia on its trip to City Hall in downtown Philadelphia via subway. This car received a general overhaul in June 1980 and as a result of a derailment at the Bethlehem Pike Loop was scrapped in October 1983. (*Kenneth C. Springirth photograph*)

On July 6, 1997, PCC car No. 2168 (same car on page 76 top picture eleven years earlier) in its special Chestnut Hill paint scheme is on a rail excursion on Route 10 on 63rd Street at Oxford Street in the Overbrook neighborhood in the northwest part of West Philadelphia. (*Kenneth C. Springirth photograph*)

Girard Avenue at 63rd Street in the Haddington neighborhood of western Philadelphia at the western end of trolley Route 15 on July 24, 1999, is the location of Route 10 (on a diversion routing) trolley No. 9065 built by Kawasaki Heavy Industries delivered on October 12, 1981 and placed in revenue on October 15, 1981. There were 112 of these 50-foot-long single-end cars (Nos. 9000–9111) built, each weighing 58,650 pounds, with a seating capacity of fifty-one, a maximum capacity of 101, and a maximum speed on level track of 50 miles per hour. (*Kenneth C. Springirth photograph*)

On October 28, 2001, Route 10 SEPTA Kawasaki Heavy Industries car No. 9075 (delivered on July 23, 1982 and placed in service on July 29, 1982) is southbound on 40th Street at Spruce Street on a diversion routing in the University City District of Philadelphia. Subway Surface Routes 10, 11, 13, 34, and 36 use applicable portions of the diversion routing when the subway is shut down for major repair, maintenance, or some other obstruction. (*Kenneth C. Springirth photograph*)

SEPTA Kawasaki PCC II car No. 2331 (original PCC car No. 2758 departed from Luzerne Depot on November 4, 2002 and was rebuilt by Brookville Equipment Corporation and returned as PCC II car No. 2331 on July 30, 2004) on February 4, 2006 is going into service leaving Callowhill Depot located on the southwest corner of the 5900 block of Callowhill Street in the Carroll Park neighborhood of West Philadelphia. (*Kenneth C. Springirth photograph*)

On June 24, 1999, Route 11 Kawasaki car No. 9002 (delivered June 4, 1981 and placed in service on July 14, 1981) is crossing CSX Transportation Railroad track on Main Street at 6th Street in Borough of Darby, Delaware County, Pennsylvania. In Tampa, Florida, CSX has another example of its railroad line crossing a streetcar line where the TECO Streetcar Line track between Ybor City and Tampa Union Station crosses a CSX line. (*Kenneth C. Springirth photograph*)

Route 11 Kawasaki car No. 9098 (delivered March 26, 1982 and placed in service on April 1, 1982) is turning from 42nd Street diversion trackage to its regular route on Woodland Avenue on August 15, 2014. From 10 p.m. on Friday August 1, 2014 through 4 a.m. on Monday August 18, 2014, trolley routes 10, 11, 13, 34, and 36 did not operate in the Center City subway; however, they began and ended at 40th and Market Streets. SEPTA's Track Department welded long rail strings and installed more than 14,000 feet of new rail on the eastbound track of the tunnel from the Portal to 22nd Street. SEPTA's power department replaced almost 24,000 feet of worn overhead contact wire (the wire that provides electricity to move trolleys). (*Kenneth C. Springirth photograph*)

On 10th Street near Main Street in the borough of Darby in Delaware County, Pennsylvania, SEPTA PCC II car No. 2320 (original PCC car No. 2750 departed from Elmwood Depot on February 25, 2002 and was rebuilt by Brookville Equipment Corporation and returned as PCC II car No. 2320 on September 9, 2003) is on a special October 18, 2008 OC Trolley Fest celebrating the area's trolley transportation. This event was created by husband-and-wife team John and Jan Haigis to bring attention to Darby's rail heritage. (*Kenneth C. Springirth photograph*)

Route 13 SEPTA Kawasaki car No. 9004 (delivered on June 10, 1981 and placed in service on July 16, 1981) is on Main Street passing the Darby Loop in Darby, Pennsylvania, on October 18, 2008. There are 112 single-end 50-foot-long Kawasaki cars on the city routes (Nos. 9000–9111) weighing 57,882 pounds, maximum speed on level ground of 50 miles per hour, and have a trolley pole for power collection. (*Kenneth C. Springirth photograph*)

Kawasaki car No. 9062 (delivered on October 7, 1981 and placed in service on October 15, 1981) is on Chester Avenue at Allen Drive passing by the Yeadon Loop in the borough of Yeadon, Delaware County, Pennsylvania, on July 4, 1999. Trolley Route 62 (Darby–Yeadon) ended in January 1971 with certain trolley Route 13 trips extended to Darby. (*Kenneth C. Springirth photograph*)

Eight years later, Route 13 Kawasaki car No. 9062 (same car as top picture in a simplified paint scheme) is on Chester Avenue at 49th Street, on October 20, 2007. This is the Cedar Park neighborhood of West Philadelphia that was originally farmland that developed as a streetcar suburb initially with the building of horsecar lines in the 1850s and with the arrival of electric trolley car lines in 1892. (*Kenneth C. Springirth photograph*)

In the University City District of Philadelphia, on October 27, 2001, SEPTA Route 13 Kawasaki car No. 9016 (delivered on November 19, 1982 and placed in service on January 31, 1982) is on 40th Street south of Market Street. (*Kenneth C. Springirth photograph*)

On August 15, 2014, SEPTA Route 13 Kawasaki car No. 9078 (delivered on October 5, 1982 and placed in service on November 2, 1982) is turning from 42nd Street onto Chester Avenue in the University City District of Philadelphia. This diversion trackage was used when the trolley subway was shut down during a maintenance blitz. (*Kenneth C. Springirth photograph*)

On August 15, 2014, SEPTA Route 13 Kawasaki car No. 9028 (delivered on March 31, 1982 and placed in service on April 14, 1982) is on Chester Avenue at 43rd Street in the Spruce Hill neighborhood in the University City District of West Philadelphia. (*Kenneth C. Springirth photograph*)

SEPTA Richmond Street and Westmoreland Street Loop on February 28, 1964 in the Bridesburg neighborhood of Philadelphia is the location from left to right of Route 15 car No. 2108 (delivered in August 1948 and scrapped in 1979 [one of fifty PCC cars, Nos. 2091–2140, built by St. Louis Car Company powered by four Westinghouse type 1432J motors]), and Route 60 car No. 2180 (delivered in July 1948 and destroyed in the Woodland carbarn fire of October 1975 [one of sixty PCC cars, Nos. 2141–2200, built by St. Louis Car Company powered by four General Electric type 1220A motors]). (*Kenneth C. Springirth photograph*)

Blackpool, England, "Boat Trolley" is at the SEPTA Route 15 Richmond and Cumberland Loop in Philadelphia on August 6, 1977. This was one of twelve Boat Trolleys (Nos. 225–236) built by English Electric in Preston, England, during 1934–1935. Four Boat Trolleys were scrapped in 1968, and the eight remaining Boat Trolleys were renumbered 600–607 in 1968. Boat Trolley No. 603 (original No. 228) went to SEPTA in Philadelphia. It was regauged to fit Philadelphia's 5-foot 2.5-inch track gauge. In 1984, it was sold to San Francisco Municipal Railway and renumbered back to its original No. 228. (*Kenneth C. Springirth photograph*)

On July 13, 1992, at the Richmond Street & Westmoreland Street Loop, SEPTA Route 15 PCC car No. 2104 is waiting for departure time. This car was built in August 1948 by St. Louis Car Company, received a general overhaul in November 1982, and was sold to the Middletown & Hummelstown Railroad in May 1994. (*Kenneth C. Springirth photograph*)

SEPTA Route 15 Kawasaki car No. 9096 (delivered on March 31, 1982 and placed in service on April 5, 1982) is at the Richmond Street and Westmoreland Street Loop on a sunny August 23, 1995. Kawasaki trolleys operated on Route 15 from June 18, 1995 to September 9, 1995 because of a Philadelphia Water Department project at 48th Street and Lancaster Avenue. (*Kenneth C. Springirth photograph*)

Crossing the Schuylkill River via the Girard Avenue Bridge on July 4, 1999 from left to right are Kawasaki car No. 9073 (delivered on July 19, 1982 and placed in service on July 22, 1982) and Peter Witt type car No. 8534 (one of fifty single-end cars [Nos. 8485–8534] ordered on January 30, 1926 from J. G. Brill Company and delivered during April 20, 1926 to May 25, 1926). Since 1999, No. 8534 has been preserved at the Electric City Trolley Museum at Scranton, Pennsylvania. (*Kenneth C. Springirth photograph*)

On October 15, 2006, SEPTA Route 15 Kawasaki car No. 9000 (first car delivered on July 23, 1980 and placed in service on November 3, 1980) is on Richmond Street at Cumberland Street. This portion of streetcar Route 15 on Richmond Street from Cumberland Street to Cambria Street is parallel to the elevated Interstate 95 expressway. (*Kenneth C. Springirth photograph*)

Westbound SEPTA Route 15 PCC II car No. 2329 (original PCC car No. 2182 departed Luzerne Depot on October 3, 2002 and was rebuilt by Brookville Equipment Corporation and returned as PCC II car No. 2329 on June 23, 2004) is on South College Avenue west of Corinthian Avenue on January 2, 2006 in the Fairmount neighborhood of Philadelphia passing by Founders Hall of Girard College with its Greek Revival architecture characterized by its Corinthian columns forming an elaborate front entrance. (*Kenneth C. Springirth photograph*)

On January 1, 2006, Girard Avenue at Corinthian Avenue is the location of westbound SEPTA Route 15 PCC II car No. 2337 (original PCC car No. 2783 departed Luzerne Depot on February 6, 2003 and returned as PCC II car No. 2337 on November 23, 2004). This location is about 3 miles from downtown Philadelphia. (*Kenneth C. Springirth photograph*)

The next day, January 2, 2006, the above SEPTA Route 15 PCC II car No. 2337 was photographed eastbound at 26th Street and Poplar Street in the Fairmount neighborhood of Philadelphia. (*Kenneth C. Springirth photograph*)

Westbound SEPTA Route 15 PCC II car No. 2324 (original PCC car No. 2777 departed Luzerne Depot on June 20, 2002 and returned as PCC II car No. 2324 on March 26, 2004) is at 25th Street and Poplar Street on January 1, 2006 in the Fairmount neighborhood of Philadelphia which is close to Fairmount Park. (*Kenneth C. Springirth photograph*)

Westbound Route 15 PCC II car No. 2333 (original PCC car No. 2746 departed from Luzerne Depot on December 5, 2002 and was rebuilt by Brookville Equipment Corporation and returned as PCC II car No. 2333 on September 14, 2004) is westbound on Girard Avenue at North 6th Street in the Northern Liberties neighborhood of Philadelphia on January 2, 2006. (*Kenneth C. Springirth photograph*)

At Girard Avenue crossing 60th Street (used by the former Route 46 trolley line that used double-ended trolley cars was converted to bus operation on August 11, 1957) in the Haddington neighborhood of West Philadelphia, on February 3, 2007, is the location of SEPTA Route 15 PCC II car No. 2325 (original PCC car No. 2741 departed from Germantown Depot on August 8, 2002 and was rebuilt by Brookville Equipment Corporation and returned as PCC II car No. 2325 on April 14, 2004). (*Kenneth C. Springirth photograph*)

On February 3, 2007, SEPTA Route 15 PCC II car No. 2326 (original PCC car No. 2197 departed from Luzerne Depot on August 28, 2002 and was rebuilt by Brookville Equipment Corporation and returned as PCC II car No. 2326 on April 28, 2004) is on Girard Avenue at 62nd Street in the Haddington neighborhood of West Philadelphia. (*Kenneth C. Springirth photograph*)

On May 19, 2007, Route 15 PCC II car No. 2337 (original PCC car No. 2783 departed from Luzerne Depot on February 6, 2003 and was rebuilt by Brookville Equipment Corporation and returned as PCC II car No. 2337 on November 23, 2004) is on Richmond Street at Madison Street turning into the Richmond Street and Westmoreland Street Loop in the Richmond neighborhood of Philadelphia. (*Kenneth C. Springirth photograph*)

Westbound SEPTA Route 15 PCC II car No. 2331 (original PCC car No. 2758 departed from Luzerne Depot on November 4, 2002 and was rebuilt by Brookville Equipment Corporation and returned as PCC II car No. 2331 on July 30, 2004) is on Girard Avenue at Front Street in the Fishtown neighborhood of Philadelphia on October 19, 2007. (*Kenneth C. Springirth photograph*)

On June 8, 2009, Route 15 PCC II car No. 2320 (original car No. 2750 departed from Elmwood Depot on February 25, 2002 and was rebuilt by Brookville Equipment Corporation and returned as PCC II car No. 2320 on September 9, 2003) is at the Richmond and Westmoreland Loop in the Richmond neighborhood of Philadelphia. (*Kenneth C. Springirth photograph*)

On a cloudy bright February 5, 2010, Route 15 PCC II car No. 2323 (original PCC car No. 2798 departed from Luzerne Depot on July 15, 2002 and was rebuilt by Brookville Equipment Corporation and returned as PCC II car No. 2323 on March 11, 2004) is on Girard Avenue at Columbia Avenue in the Fishtown neighborhood of Philadelphia. (*Kenneth C. Springirth photograph*)

On February 5, 2010, Route 15 PCC II car No. 2328 (original PCC car No. 2726 departed from Luzerne Depot on September 23, 2002 and was rebuilt by Brookville Equipment Corporation and returned as PCC II car No. 2328 on May 27, 2004) is on Girard Avenue at Marlborough Street in the Fishtown neighborhood of Philadelphia. (*Kenneth C. Springirth photograph*)

Westbound Route 15 PCC II car No. 2322 (original PCC car Nc. 2770 departed from Luzerne Depot on February 27, 2002 and was rebuilt by Brookville Equipment Corporation and returned as PCC II car No. 2322 on January 29, 2004) is on Girard Avenue at Susquehanna Avenue in the Fishtown neighborhood of Philadelphia. (*Kenneth C. Springirth photograph*)

In the Port Richmond neighborhood of Philadelphia, SEPTA Route 15 PCC II car No. 2335 (original PCC car No. 2158 departed from Luzerne Depot on January 2, 2003 and was rebuilt by Brookville Equipment Corporation and returned as PCC II car No. 2335 on October 19, 2004) is on Richmond Street at Ann Street on August 6, 2010. (*Kenneth C. Springirth photograph*)

On August 6, 2010, SEPTA Route 15 PCC II car No. 2320 (original PCC car No. 2750 departed from Elmwood Depot on February 25, 2002 and was rebuilt by Brookville Equipment Corporation returning as PCC II car No. 2320 on September 9, 2003) is on Girard Avenue at Palmer Street in the Fishtown neighborhood of Philadelphia. (*Kenneth C. Springirth photograph*)

Girard Avenue at Front Street on September 15, 2012, in the Fishtown neighborhood north of Center City, Philadelphia, is the location of Route 15 PCC II car No. 2334 (original PCC car No. 2753 departed from Luzerne Depot on December 19, 2002 and was rebuilt by Brookville Equipment Corporation and returned as PCC II car No. 2334 on September 24, 2004). (*Kenneth C. Springirth photograph*)

On September 15, 2012 in Philadelphia's Fishtown neighborhood, SEPTA Route 15 PCC II car No. 2325 is leaving the Route 15 Frankford Avenue and Delaware Avenue Loop while, on the left, Route 15 PCC II car No. 2334 is on Frankford Avenue preparing to turn onto Delaware Avenue to enter the loop and behind it in the distance on Frankford Avenue is another Route 15 PCC II car. (*Kenneth C. Springirth photograph*)

On June 11, 2018, Route 15 PCC II car No. 2327 (original PCC car No. 2747 departed from Luzerne Depot on September 9, 2002 and was rebuilt by Brookville Equipment Corporation and returned as PCC II car No. 2327 on May 13, 2004) is on a layover at the Frankford Avenue and Delaware Avenue Loop in the Fishtown neighborhood of Philadelphia. (*Kenneth C. Springirth photograph*)

On July 20, 1966, Philadelphia Transportation Company (PTC) PCC car No. 2799 (delivered in April 1947, received a general overhaul by SEPTA in August 1985, repainted as Philadelphia Suburban "Red Arrow," went to Lancaster, PA, and in 2012 to Warren Rail Car in Warren, Pennsylvania) is southbound on 12th Street at Walnut Street in downtown Philadelphia. This was one of seventy-five cars (Nos. 2726–2800) built by St. Louis Car Company, each powered by four General Electric type 1220A motors. (*Kenneth C. Springirth photograph*)

PTC PCC car No. 2760 is at the Route 23 southern terminus at 10th Street and Bigler Street in the Stadium District neighborhood of South Philadelphia on March 4, 1962. This car was delivered in March 1947 (one of seventy-five cars [Nos. 2726–2800] all electric built by St. Louis Car Company), received a general overhaul by SEPTA in February 1984, and was sold to a private individual in October 1996. (*Kenneth C. Springirth photograph*)

Northbound PTC Route 23 PCC car No. 2736 (delivered in March 1947) is northbound on 11th Street at Market Street in the heart of downtown Philadelphia on July 20, 1966. This car was hit by car No. 2625 on Germantown Avenue on January 7, 1977 and was scrapped in 1979. (*Kenneth C. Springirth photograph*)

On August 8, 1985, SEPTA Route 23 PCC car No. 2143 (delivered in June 1948 and received a general overhaul in July 1985) is northbound on 11th at Snyder Avenue in the East Passyunk Crossing neighborhood of South Philadelphia. This was one of sixty "all electric" cars (Nos. 2141–2200) built by St. Louis Car Company and delivered June–August 1948, with each powered by four GE type 1220A motors. (*Kenneth C. Springirth photograph*)

Chestnut Hill Loop in the Chestnut Hill neighborhood of Philadelphia on March 28, 1987 is the location of SEPTA PCC car No. 2110 (delivered in August 1948, received a general overhaul in August 1981, and sold to San Francisco Municipal Railway in October 1992 with restoration by Morrison-Knudsen in 1993, repainted to commemorate Los Angeles Railway and renumbered 1052). This was one of fifty cars (Nos. 2091–2140) originally built by St. Louis Car Company and delivered August–September 1948. (*Kenneth C. Springirth photograph*)

Buses had permanently replaced Route 23 trolleys on February 27, 1992. However, weekend trolley service was restored on the Chestnut Hill portion of the line on Germantown Avenue from Westview Avenue to Bethlehem Pike from September 13, 1992 until June 15, 1996. Germantown Avenue at Bethlehem Pike in the Chestnut Hill neighborhood of Philadelphia on October 4, 1992 is the location of Route 23 PCC car No. 2785 (delivered in April 1947, received a general overhaul in August 1986, was the Chestnut Hill trolley from 1992 to 1996, sold to Glen Echo Park, Maryland in 2005, and in 2010 was sold to San Diego Vintage Trolley and renumbered 533). (*Kenneth C. Springirth photograph*)

On August 22, 1993, PCC car No. 2785 (same car shown in above picture) is at the Germantown Depot, repainted with the Chestnut Hill trolley insignia on the side. (*Kenneth C. Springirth photograph*)

Chestnut Hill Loop is the location of Chestnut Hill trolley No. 2750 on August 22, 1993. This car was delivered by St. Louis Car Company in 1947, received a general overhaul in June 1986, was the Chestnut Hill Trolley from 1992 to 1996, and was rebuilt by Brookville Equipment Corporation and returned as PCC II car No. 2320 on September 9, 2003 as shown in the top picture on page 80. (*Kenneth C. Springirth photograph*)

On October 21, 1995, SEPTA PCC car No. 2732 (delivered in March 1947, received a general overhaul in February 1985, repainted green with pinstripes in 1995, in 2005 sold to Glen Echo Park in Maryland, and in 2012 sold to General Machine & Tool Company in Cheverly, Maryland) is on 12th Street at Filbert Street in downtown Philadelphia on tourist-oriented Route 51 that operated sporadically during 1995 and 1996. This was one of seventy-five PCC cars built by St. Louis Car Company (Nos. 2726–2800) delivered during March–April 1947. (*Kenneth C. Springirth photograph*)

On October 22, 1995, SEPTA PCC car No. 2728 (followed by Kawasaki car No. 9045) is northbound on 11th Street at Filbert Street in downtown Philadelphia working a Route 51 trip that was a short-lived effort to operate a tourist-oriented streetcar service from downtown Philadelphia to the Philadelphia Zoo using portions of Route 15 and Route 23 trackage. This car, originally delivered during March 1947, received a general overhaul in May 1986, was painted silver in 1995, in 2005 went to Baltimore Streetcar Museum, later Lancaster, Pennsylvania, and in 2012 to Warren Rail Car in Warren, Pennsylvania. *(Kenneth C. Springirth photograph)*

Already dressed up for the holiday season, SEPTA PCC car No. 2799 is northbound on 11th Street at Walnut Street in downtown Philadelphia on November 27, 1998. There were 100 of these PCC cars ordered for Route 23 in July 1944. The first twenty-five (Nos. 2701–2725) were each equipped with four Westinghouse type 1432D motors. The last seventy-five (Nos. 2726–2800) were each equipped with four General Electric type 1220A motors. *(Kenneth C. Springirth photograph)*

Repainted in an attractive orange below the windows, white roof and horizontal blue stripes, SEPTA PCC car No. 2632 is at the 49th and Woodland depot waiting for the next assignment in 1977. This was one of ten cars (Nos. 2624–2633) ordered in April 1941 and delivered in June 1942 from St. Louis Car Company with each car having four Westinghouse type 1432D motors. (*Kenneth C. Springirth photograph*)

On August 7, 1994, SEPTA PCC car No. 2726 (delivered in March 1947, received a general overhaul in April 1987, and years later after this picture was taken was rebuilt by Brookville Equipment Corporation returning on May 27, 2004 as car No. 2328) on the siding and Route 34 Kawasaki car No. 9096 (delivered on March 31, 1982 and placed in service on April 5, 1982) are at 40th Street and Woodland Avenue in the Woodland Terrace neighborhood near the 40th Street trolley tunnel used by trolley routes 11, 13, 34, and 36 in West Philadelphia. (*Kenneth C. Springirth photograph*)

At the 40th Street trolley tunnel on July 24, 1999, PCC car No. 2168 (delivered from St. Louis Car Company in July 1948, received a general overhaul in January 1986, was the Chestnut Hill Trolley during 1992–1996, and sold to the Baltimore Streetcar Museum in 2005) is ready to exit the tunnel, while Kawasaki car No. 9071 (delivered March 26, 1982 and placed in service on April 1, 1982) is entering the tunnel. (*Kenneth C. Springirth photograph*)

On a sunny winter January 29, 2000, with snow on the ground, SEPTA Route 34 PCC car No. 2732 looks beautiful on Baltimore Avenue at 54th Street in the Angora neighborhood of Southwest Philadelphia. This car looked just as good as it was in downtown Philadelphia on October 21, 1995 shown on page 6 in this book. (*Kenneth C. Springirth photograph*)

SEPTA Route 34 Kawasaki car No. 9032 (delivered on April 16, 1982 and placed in service on April 21, 1982) is eastbound for downtown Philadelphia on Baltimore Avenue at 45th Street in the Spruce Hill neighborhood of West Philadelphia on June 11, 2018. This neighborhood was built as a streetcar suburb whose growth and development were strongly shaped by using the streetcar system as the primary means of transportation. (*Kenneth C. Springirth photograph*)

On March 18, 1962, Philadelphia Transportation Company Route 36 PCC car No. 2591 (delivered in May 1942 and scrapped in 1981) is at the 94th Street and Eastwick Avenue loop in the Eastwick neighborhood of southwest Philadelphia waiting for departure time. This was part of group of forty-three PCC cars (Nos. 2581–2623) built by St. Louis Car Company and delivered in May–June 1942 each powered by four General Electric type 1198 motors. (*Kenneth C. Springirth photograph*)

The northbound 38th Street diversion trackage south of Market Street in the University City District of Philadelphia finds Route 36 Kawasaki car No. 9067 (delivered on October 14, 1981 and placed in service on October 19, 1981) heading for 40th and Market Street on February 5, 2006. (*Kenneth C. Springirth photograph*)

Route 36 Kawasaki car No. 9031 (delivered on September 30, 1981 and placed in service on October 7 1981) has arrived at the 80th and Eastwick Avenue terminus on March 21, 2004. While Route 36 is the longest of the five subway-surface lines, trolley car service once operated from downtown Philadelphia to the Westinghouse plant in Essington, Pennsylvania. However, it was cut back to 94th Street and Eastwick Avenue on September 9, 1956; cut back to 88th and Eastwick Avenue on August 15, 1962; and cut back to 80th and Eastwick Avenue on April 26, 1975. (*Kenneth C. Springirth photograph*)

On August 15, 2014, with a colorful advertisement, Route 36 Kawasaki car No. 9107 (delivered on March 19, 1982 and placed in service on March 22,1982) is on the diversion trackage on 42nd Street south of Spruce Street (used when the subway is closed for maintenance or other purposes) in the University City District in West Philadelphia. (*Kenneth C. Springirth photograph*)

SEPTA PCC III car No. 2332 (originally PCC car No. 2196 that departed from Luzerne Depot on November 18, 2002, rebuilt by Brookville Equipment Corporation, and returned as PCC II car No. 2332 on August 24, 2004) completely rebuilt by Woodland Shop is at the Elmwood Carhouse for its fortieth anniversary event on September 15, 2021. The Elmwood Carhouse opened on November 15, 1981 replacing the Woodland Carhouse that was damaged by the October 23, 1975 fire. However, Woodland became SEPTA's rebuilding facility and during 2020–2024 was reconstructing piece by piece eighteen PCC cars for the Route 15 Girard Avenue line. (*Bill Monaghan photograph*)

On September 15, 2021 at the Elmwood Carhouse, SEPTA celebrated Elmwood Carhouse's fortieth anniversary. For this special event, Kawasaki car No. 9093 (delivered on November 6, 1981 and placed in service on November 10, 1981) was wrapped featuring photos of various views of SEPTA's trolley cars taken by SEPTA employee Edward Springer. (*Bill Monaghan photograph*)

As part of the Elmwood Depot's fortieth anniversary, SEPTA operated a special charter using Kawasaki car No. 9093 from Elmwood Depot via Route 36 to the 80th and Elmwood Avenue terminus at the southern edge of the Penrose Plaza Shopping Center parking lot shown in the above photograph. (*Bill Monaghan photograph*)

Southbound Philadelphia Transportation Company (PTC) Route 47 PCC car No. 2124 (built by St. Louis Car Company, delivered in August 1948, received a general overhaul in August 1980, and in 1982 sold to San Francisco Municipal Railway where it was refurbished, repainted in Chicago Transit Authority green and cream and renumbered 1058 by Morrison-Knudsen in 1993) is on 5th Street at Wyoming Avenue in the Feltonville neighborhood of North Philadelphia on May 31, 1968. (*Kenneth C. Springirth photograph*)

On May 31, 1968, PTC Route 47 PCC car No. 2143 (built by St. Louis Car Company, delivered in June 1948, received a general overhaul in July 1985, and was sold to Brookville Equipment Corporation in 2004) is on 5th Street between Lindley Avenue and Duncannon Avenue in the Olney neighborhood of North Philadelphia. (*Kenneth C. Springirth photograph*)

PTC Route 50 car No. 2287 (originally No. 799 one of seventy-five "all electric" cars [Nos. 725–799] built and delivered during March–August 1946 by St. Louis Car Company [each having four Westinghouse type 1432 motors] for Kansas City Public Service Company of which forty cars were purchased by PTC, repainted, and renumbered 2251–2290) is on Wyoming Avenue at 3rd Street in the Feltonville neighborhood of North Philadelphia on May 31, 1968. This car was scrapped in October 1972. (*Kenneth C. Springirth photograph*)

On August 13, 1976, SEPTA Route 50 car No. 2252 is southbound on 4th Street at Chestnut Street in downtown Philadelphia on August 13, 1976. This was originally Kansas City Public Service Company No. 728 and was purchased by PTC, repainted (with Delaware painted on the side to honor that bicentennial state), and renumbered 2252. This car was scrapped in December 1982. (*Kenneth C. Springirth photograph*)

SEPTA Route 53 car No. 2310 is at the Route 53 Loop at 10th Street and Luzerne Street in the Hunting Park neighborhood of Philadelphia waiting for departure time on July 22, 1979. PCC car No. 2310 (originally Birmingham Electric Company PCC car No. 829) one of forty-eight cars (Nos. 800–847) that were all-electric cars each with four Westinghouse type 1432 motors delivered by Pullman Company during November 1946 to January 1947. They were sold to the Toronto Transit Commission (TTC), delivered in 1952, and renumbered 4700–4747, with No. 829 becoming No. 4728. Nineteen of these cars were sold to SEPTA. They were delivered in April 1976 and renumbered 2300–2318, with No. 829 becoming SEPTA 2310. Scrapping of the nineteen former TTC cars began in 1979, and during 1982, the remaining six cars (Nos. 2300, 2304, 2307, 2310, 2311, and 2317) were scrapped. (*Kenneth C. Springirth photograph*)

On April 27, 1968, Philadelphia Transportation Company (PTC) Route 56 car No. 2551 (delivered in January 1941 and destroyed in the Woodland Carbarn fire of October 1975) is on Erie Avenue at Kensington Avenue in the Juniata Park neighborhood of Philadelphia. This was one of eighty cars (Nos. 2501–2580) built by St. Louis Car Company delivered in December 1940–February 1941, with each car having four General Electric type 1198F3 motors. (*Kenneth C. Springirth photograph*)

In the Wissinoming neighborhood of Philadelphia on June 19, 1980, SEPTA Route 56 car No. 2277 is on Torresdale Avenue at Benner Street. This car was originally Kansas City Public Service Company (KCPS) of Kansas City, Missouri, car No. 729 (one of seventy-five PCC cars (Nos. 725–799) built by St. Louis Car Company and delivered March–August 1946). KCPS sold forty PCC cars to PTC in 1955 that were repainted and renumbered 2251–2290. (*Kenneth C. Springirth photograph*)

SEPTA Route 56 car No. 2156 is pulling out of the Torresdale Avenue and Cottman Avenue Loop in the Tacony Neighborhood of Northeast Philadelphia on May 29, 1992. This car was delivered by St. Louis Car Company in June 1948, received a general overhaul in September 1983, and was sold to Brookville Equipment Corporation in 2004. (*Kenneth C. Springirth photograph*)

Leaving the Route 56 Torresdale Avenue and Cottman Avenue loop on May 29, 1992 is car No. 2730. This car was delivered by St. Louis Car Company in March 1947 and received a general overhaul in May 1986. After this picture was taken, this car was sent for rebuilding to Brookville Equipment Corporation on October 17, 2002, and was returned on July 14, 2004 as car No. 2330. (*Kenneth C. Springirth photograph*)

On May 29, 1992, SEPTA Route 56 PCC car No. 2733 (built by St. Louis Car Company and delivered in March 1947 and received a general overhaul in October 1986) is on Torresdale Avenue at Fraley Street in the Wissinoming neighborhood of Northeast Philadelphia. On September 1995, this car was placed on static display where it can be closely viewed inside at the SEPTA Headquarters at 1234 Market Street in Center City, Philadelphia. (*Kenneth C. Springirth photograph*)

On August 6, 1977, SEPTA Route 60 car No. 2305 is preparing to turn from Allegheny Avenue onto Richmond Street a short distance away from its eastern terminus at Richmond Street and Westmoreland Street in the Richmond neighborhood of Philadelphia. This car was originally No. 811, built by Pullman Company (one of forty-eight delivered between November 1946 and January 1947) for Birmingham Electric Company. The forty-eight cars were sold to the Toronto Transit Commission (TTC), delivered in 1952, and renumbered 4700–4747, with No. 811 becoming No. 4711. It was sold to SEPTA, delivered in April 1976, renumbered 2305, and scrapped in October 1981. SEPTA replaced Route 60 trolleys with buses on September 4, 1977. *(Kenneth C. Springirth photograph)*

On June 2, 1963, PTC Route 62 (Yeadon–Darby shuttle route) PCC car No. 2631 is on Main Street in the borough of Darby in Delaware County, Pennsylvania. Delivered in June 1942 from St. Louis Car Company, this was the first trolley to enter the 40th Street portal of the subway-surface extension at 4:50 a.m. on October 17, 1955. On January 24, 1971, SEPTA replaced Route 62 by an extension of certain Route 13 trolley trips from Yeadon to Darby. *(Kenneth C. Springirth photograph)*

3

Suburban Philadelphia Trolley Car History

The Philadelphia & West Chester Traction Company (PWCT) began trolley car service on August 15, 1895, using steam dummies, from 63rd Street in Philadelphia to Newtown Square. Electric trolley car service took over the line on May 6, 1896, and service was extended to West Chester on December 17, 1898. Trackage from 63rd Street to 69th Street was used from 1896 to when the 69th Street Terminal was opened in 1907. On May 29, 1902, the Ardmore and Llanerch Street Railway began trolley car service from 63rd Street to Ardmore. Trolley car service from 63rd Street to Baltimore Avenue in Clifton Heights opened March 15, 1905, was extended to the Clifton–Aldan Train Station on April 30, 1907, extended to Providence Road in Aldan on June 30, 1907, and to Mac Dade Boulevard on July 15, 1907, and with completion of a bridge under the Baltimore & Ohio Railroad, the line was opened to Sharon Hill on August 1, 1917. Trolley service to Media opened on April 1, 1913. The Philadelphia & West Chester Traction Company and Philadelphia & Garrettford Street Railway merged into the Philadelphia Suburban Transportation Company (PSTC) on April 13, 1936. Plans by the Pennsylvania Highway Department to widen West Chester Pike resulted in the abandonment of 15.5 miles of track from Westgate Hills to West Chester with buses replacing trolley cars on June 4, 1954. The 3.5-mile section from 69th Street Terminal to West Gate Hills had rush-hour trolley service until it was abandoned on August 23,1958. Buses replaced trolley cars on the Ardmore line on December 30, 1966. On January 29, 1970, the Southeastern Pennsylvania Transportation Authority SEPTA took over PSTC.

Route 101 Media

Media Line (Route 101) and Route 102 Sharon Hill operate from the 69th Street Terminal and share about 2 miles of trackage on their predominately private right of way to Drexel Hill Junction. Route 101 continues on its own right of way west and southwest through Drexel Hill and Springfield.

Route 102 Sharon Hill

Sharon Hill Line (Route 102) runs double track southeast from Drexel Hill Junction through Drexel Hill and Clifton Heights and enters Springfield Road in Clifton Heights, Woodlawn Avenue in Aldan, and south of North Street in Collingdale returns to single track to the end of the line.

On West Chester Pike at Hawthorn Road in the census-designated place of Broomall in Marple Township, Delaware County, Pennsylvania, Philadelphia Suburban Transportation Company (PSTC) car No. 78, operating on the West Chester line, is picking up a passenger on June 3, 1954. This was one of ten lightweight "Master Unit"-style cars (Nos. 77–86) (constructed of aluminum, each car weighed 41,980 pounds, and was powered by four GE type 301B motors) built by J. G. Brill Company in 1932. This car was acquired by the Pennsylvania Trolley Museum in 1982. (*Richard Short photograph*)

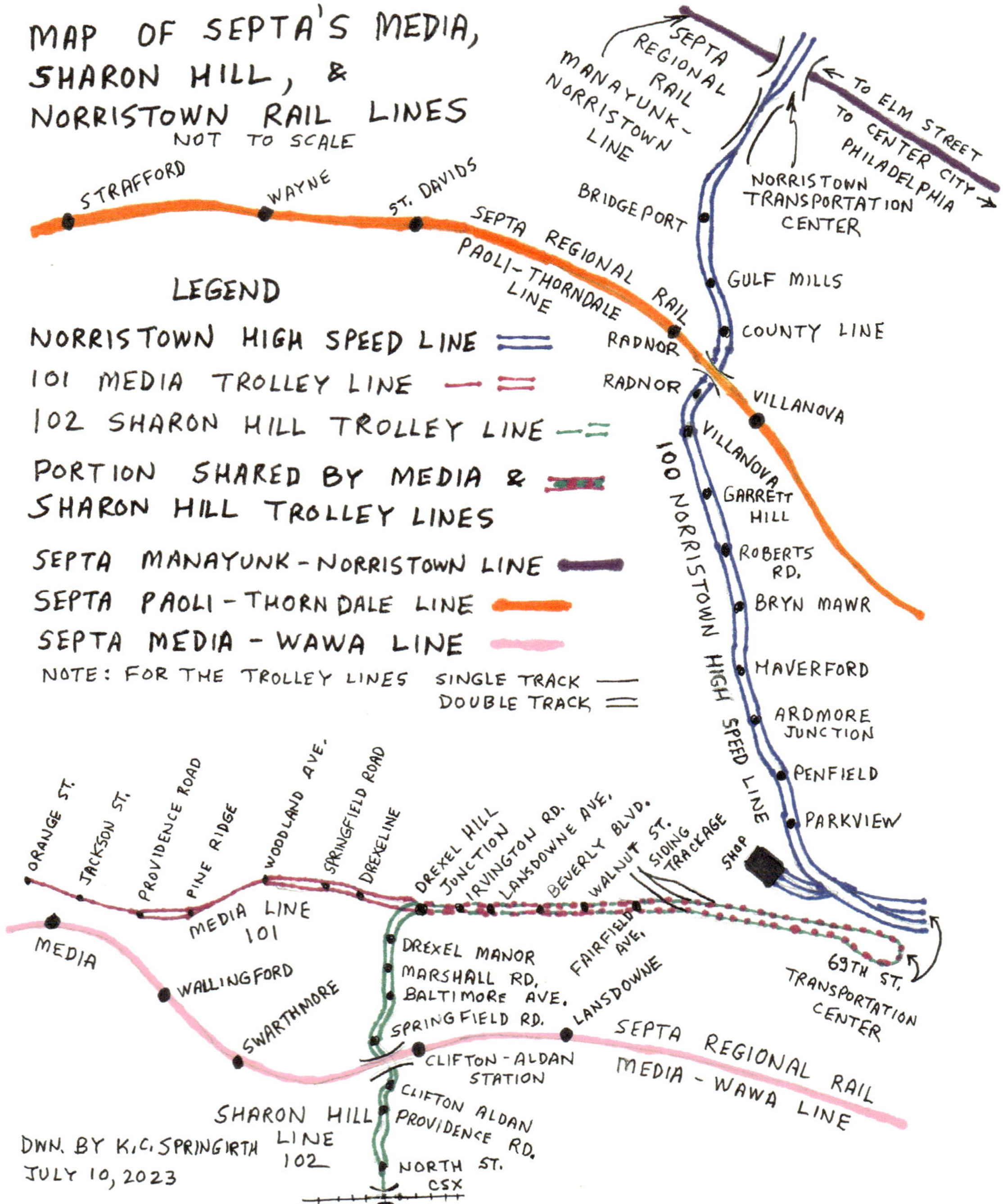

This map shows SEPTA's 13.4-mile Route 100 Norristown High Speed Line, 8.6-mile Route 101 Media Line, and 5.3-mile Route 102 Sharon Hill Line. The Media–Wawa Line crosses over the Sharon Hill Trolley Line at Clifton–Aldan Station, and the Media Train Station is within walking distance from the Media Trolley Line in Media. The Paoli–Thorndale line's Radnor and Villanova Stations are within walking distance from the Norristown Line's Radnor and Villanova Stations. The Manayunk–Norristown Line crosses under the Norristown Line at the Norristown Transportation Center.

Two passengers are about to board PSTC car No. 7 (one of ten Brilliners [Nos. 1–10] built by J. G. Brill Company in 1941, with each powered by four Westinghouse type 1433 motors) on West Chester Pike at Chester Road, in Chester County East of West Chester, Pennsylvania, on June 3, 1954, one day before the West Chester Line was converted to bus operation. (*Richard Short photograph*)

On June 8, 2002, SEPTA Kawasaki double-end trolleys (from left to right) No. 119 (delivered on August 20, 1982 and placed in service on August 27, 1982) and No. 112 (delivered on December 30, 1981 and placed in service on January 21, 1982) are at 69th Street Terminal parked on the tracks that store cars during rush hours, plus connect with the trolley plus subway/elevated car shops. The twenty-nine cars, used on the Media and Sharon Hill lines, are 53 foot long, weigh 60,043 pounds, power connection by pantograph, and have a top speed on level track of 62 miles per hour. (*Kenneth C. Springirth photograph*)

On December 26, 1969, PSTC (Red Arrow Lines) work car No. 07 is near the 69th Street Terminal with workers standing on its roof-mounted platform working on the overhead wire that carries the electrical current needed to power the trolleys. This car was originally built in 1911 by the Jewett Car Company as a freight car for the Philadelphia & West Chester Traction Company. When freight service ended in 1925, this car was converted into an overhead line car. The Pennsylvania Trolley Museum in Washington, Pennsylvania, acquired this car in 1996. (*Kenneth C. Springirth photograph*)

SEPTA Route 101 Drexelbrook Station on Wildell Road south of Woodland Avenue in Drexel Hill, a census-designated place, in Upper Darby Township, Delaware County, Pennsylvania, on a rail excursion is the location of PSTC car No. 84 on April 24, 1960. This was one of ten cars (Nos. 77–86), built by J. G. Brill Company in 1932, that reduced labor, power, and maintenance costs. (*Kenneth C. Springirth photograph*)

On June 30, 1977, SEPTA center door-type trolley No. 73 is on State Street for the Media Town Fair in the borough of Media county seat of Delaware County, Pennsylvania. This was one of twelve cars (Nos. 65–76) built by J. G. Brill Company in 1926. This car had been refurbished by SEPTA in 1972 for the community's business association for the promotion of Media. During the Media Town Fair, the regular Route 101 service car would transfer passengers at the edge of the business district to No. 73 for the continuation of the trip to the terminus on State Street at Orange Street in Media. In 1990, No. 73 was acquired by the Pennsylvania Trolley Museum. (*Kenneth C. Springirth photograph*)

State Street at Providence Road in Media on October 26, 1996 is the location of SEPTA Route 101 Kawasaki car No. 123 (delivered on August 27, 1982 and placed in service on September 23, 1982) with a Halloween face on the car front and 666 Transylvania Express on the front destination sign. (*Kenneth C. Springirth photograph*)

On February 1, 2014, SEPTA Kawasaki car No. 101 (delivered on September 14, 1982 and placed in service on September 29, 1982) is on a rail excursion past Paper Mill Road crossing the Smedley Park Trestle over Crum Creek on the Media Line. This car was wrapped to resemble Philadelphia & West Chester Traction Company car No. 38 (purchased from Jewett Car Company in 1913 for the Media line and scrapped in 1933) for the Media Line's 100th anniversary of its opening on April 1, 1913. (*Bill Monaghan photograph*)

On June 4, 2014, eastbound Route 101 Kawasaki car No. 126 (delivered September 3, 1982 and placed in service on October 9, 1982) is on State Street at Monroe Street in Media, Pennsylvania, for an eastbound trip to the 69th Street Transportation Center. (*Kenneth C. Springirth photograph*)

SEPTA Route 101 Kawasaki car No. 106 (delivered November 1, 1982 and placed in service on November 12, 1982) is crossing Providence Road in Media, Pennsylvania, at the Providence Road trolley station on June 4, 2014. East of this point, there is a stretch of double track where a distant trolley is waiting to pass. (*Kenneth C. Springirth photograph*)

The State Street at Orange Street terminus in Media finds Route 101 Kawasaki car No. 123 (delivered on August 27, 1982 and placed in service on September 23, 1982) and behind it training car No. 110 (delivered August 25, 1981 and placed in service on November 12, 1981) waiting for departure time on October 29, 2018. (*Kenneth C. Springirth photograph*)

SEPTA Route 101 Kawasaki car No. 122 (delivered on August 27, 1982 and placed in service on September 22, 1982) is loading passengers on Orange Street at Jackson Street in Media on October 29, 2018. Media's population trended downward from 6,444 in 1970 to 5,527 in 2010; however, it increased to 5,901 in 2020. Media is also served by SEPTA's Media/Wawa commuter rail line for direct access to downtown Philadelphia. (*Kenneth C. Springirth photograph*)

On an April 23, 1961 rail excursion, Philadelphia Suburban Transit Company vintage center door cars No. 76 and No. 66 are on the Oakview trestle over Darby Creek in Drexel Hill, a census-designated place in Upper Darby Township, Delaware County, Pennsylvania. Both cars were built by J. G. Brill Company in 1926 for the Philadelphia & West Chester Traction Company. In 1970, car No. 66 was acquired by the Pennsylvania Trolley Museum. In 1976, car No. 76 was acquired by the Electric City Trolley Museum. (*Kenneth C. Springirth photograph*)

Philadelphia Suburban Transit Company car No. 18 is at the S. Penn Street stop in Clifton Heights, a borough in Delaware County, Pennsylvania, on July 21, 1962. Weighing 49,000 pounds and powered by four Westinghouse type 1433 motors, this was one of fourteen cars (Nos. 11–24) built in 1949 by St. Louis Car Company. (*Kenneth C. Springirth photograph*)

On October 3, 2009, SEPTA Kawasaki car No. 111 (delivered on December 30, 1981 and placed in service on January 21, 1982) has left 69th Street Terminal and crossed Victory Avenue in Upper Darby Township, Delaware County, Pennsylvania, for a Route 102 trip to Sharon Hill on October 2, 2009. (*Kenneth C. Springirth photograph*)

Heading for Sharon Hill, SEPTA Route 102 car No. 121 (delivered on August 24, 1982 and placed in service on September 21, 1982) is at the Irvington Road stop (south of Hillcrest Road) in Drexel Hill, Upper Darby Township, Pennsylvania, on October 30, 2009. (*Kenneth C. Springirth photograph*)

On June 5, 2014, a two-car train composed of Kawasaki cars (from left to right) No. 113 (delivered on August 4, 1982 and placed in service on August 12, 1982) and No. 123 (delivered on August 27, 1982 and placed in service on September 23, 1982) have just crossed Turner Avenue eastbound on a school tripper on the Sharon Hill Line approaching Shadeland Avenue (Drexel Hill Junction) where the Media Line joins the Sharon Hill line, where both lines provide service to 69th Street Terminal. (*Kenneth C. Springirth photograph*)

When a portion of the Sharon Hill line was out of service from Shadeland Avenue in Drexel Hill to Sharon Hill for repair, SEPTA Kawasaki car No. 113 (delivered on August 4, 1982 and placed in service on August 12, 1982) operated as a shuttle from Shadeland Avenue to 69th Street Terminal on October 3, 2019. (*Kenneth C. Springirth photograph*)

On February 26, 2004, SEPTA Route 102 Kawasaki car No. 104 (delivered on December 4, 1982 and placed in service on December 22, 1982) is operating a rush trip as a Aldan Local from 69th Street to North Street, which is actually in the borough of Collingdale, the first station south of Aldan. (*Kenneth C. Springirth photograph*)

Woodlawn Avenue at Pennsylvania Avenue in the borough of Aldan in Delaware County, Pennsylvania, on October 29, 2018 is the location of SEPTA Route 102 Kawasaki car No.123 (delivered on August 27, 1982 and placed in service on September 23, 1982) heading for the 69th Street Transportation Center. The trolley makes a left turn onto Springfield Road and goes under the bridge of SEPTA's Regional Rail Media/Wawa commuter line and its Clifton–Aldan Station. (*Kenneth C. Springirth photograph*)

On February 26, 2004, SEPTA Route 102 Kawasaki car No. 102 (delivered on September 17, 1982 and placed in service on October 1, 1982) is at the end of the line near Chester Pike just west of High Street in the borough of Sharon Hill in Delaware County, Pennsylvania, waiting for departure time. (*Kenneth C. Springirth photograph*)

4

Norristown Line History

The Philadelphia & Western Railroad (P&W) began service on May 22, 1907 from the 69th Street Terminal in Upper Darby, a township in Delaware County, Pennsylvania, to Strafford, Pennsylvania, operating on track without any grade crossings, a maximum grade of 2.5 percent, stone ballast, 85 pound per yard rail plus most of the line was double track to enhance safety and utilization. On October 11, 1911, the line was extended 0.47 mile west to a new Strafford Line P&W station that was adjacent to the Pennsylvania Railroad's Strafford Station. A 6.3-mile line was built and opened on August 26, 1912 from Villanova Junction to Norristown. Attracting more ridership, the Norristown Line became the main line and the Strafford Line became a branch line. Lehigh Valley Transit Company (LVT) began using the P&W from 69th Street Terminal to Norristown on December 12, 1912 and used its own trackage from Norristown to Allentown.

On June 2,1930, Dr. Thomas Conway (who had taken over the faltering Chicago, Aurora & Elgin Railroad in 1922 and increased its net profit by 154 percent in four years, moved on to expand the Cincinnati, Hamilton & Dayton Railway into the Cincinnati & Lake Erie Railroad increasing its net earning 230 percent in four years) was named a director and chairman of the board to run the P&W. When P&W President Julius L. Adams died on March 1, 1931, Conway became president on April 20, 1931. After the Pennsylvania Railroad electrified its Norristown to Philadelphia commuter line and reduced travel time by up to thirteen minutes, Conway recognized the only way the P&W could increase its traffic was to speed up service. Felix Pawlowski, University of Michigan's aeronautics professor, was hired to conduct tests to reduce rail car wind resistance. His test results concluded new cars should have a clutter free roof as low as possible with flat sides, car ends shaped like a bullet, and the roof dipping down at each end. Ten double-ended Bullet cars were purchased from J. G. Brill Company. The first car, No. 200, entered 69th Street Terminal on October 27, 1931, and its brakes failed, making it crash into another older car. No one was hurt, and the car went back to Brill for rebuilding. The new cars (Nos. 200–209), costing a total of $311,440, were the first lightweight aluminum streamlined electric railway cars built in the United States. Following three days of running, the cars were withdrawn from service because of mechanical and electrical problems. On November 28, 1931, the cars were back in service.

Effective September 25, 1949, LVT no longer used P&W 69th Street to Norristown trackage and operated from the P&W Norristown Terminal to Allentown. On September 7, 1951, LVT converted their Norristown to Allentown line to bus operation. The P&W was acquired by the Philadelphia Suburban Transportation Company (PSTC) on December 31,1953. Rail service on the Strafford line ended March 23, 1956. Two Electroliners from the former Chicago North Shore & Milwaukee Railroad that ended service on January 21, 1963 were purchased at a scrapyard, refurbished with trolley poles and steps removed, updated third rail contact shoes added so that it could operate on the Norristown High Speed Line, renamed Liberty Liners, and went into service on January 31, 1964 on the former P&W 69th Street–Norristown Line. SEPTA took over PSTC on January 29, 1970.

On June 4, 1961, car No. 163 is part of a two-car train at Bryn Mawr. Originally car No. 63 (built in 1927 by J.G. Brill and powered by four Westinghouse type 535B-1 motors) was rebuilt in 1931 and became No. 163. (*Kenneth C. Springirth photograph*)

Former Chicago North Shore & Milwaukee Railroad Electroliner (one of two saved and restored as Liberty Liners) is shown on the Red Arrow Norristown Division at Villanova Junction on July 3, 1964. (*Photographer Albert J. Derr Used with permission from Audio Visual Designs [www.audiovisualdesigns.com]*)

On April 27, 1968, Philadelphia Suburban Transportation Company car No. 163 (originally built in 1931 by J.G. Brill Company as No. 63 for the Philadelphia & Western Railway [P&W]) is at the 69th Street Yard waiting for the next assignment. This car was one of eight rebuilt in 1931 and became No. 163. The rebuilding included reconstruction of the truck bolster and reduction of the wheel diameter to lower the car floor height plus rewinding the motors with both items achieving an increase in the car's maximum speed from 44 to 68 miles per hour. (*Kenneth C. Springirth photograph*)

In the lineup of former P&W cars at 69th Street Terminal, car No. 170 is waiting for the next assignment on April 27, 1968. Car No. 170 was wrecked in a collision at Ardmore Avenue with Liberty Liner "Independence Hall" on January 17, 1969 and was scrapped in 1970. (*Kenneth C. Springirth photograph*)

A three-car train of Brill "Bullet" cars pose for pictures during a November 1971 excursion. SEPTA took over PSTC on January 29, 1970. (*Photographer William J. Myers Used with permission from Audio Visual Designs [www.audiovisualdesigns.com]*)

On July 23, 1976, Radnor Station in Radnor Township, Delaware County, Pennsylvania, is the location of Bullet car No. 207, one of ten (Nos. 200–209) built by Brill in 1931, with each car powered by four GE type 706B-2 motors. (*Kenneth C. Springirth photograph*)

On May 20, 2007, Radnor Station is the location of Norristown High Speed Line car No. 155, one of twenty-six unique type N-5 (they are the fifth car type since the line opened to Norristown on August 26, 1912) standard-gauge cars (Nos. 130–155) built by Asea Brown Boveri Traction (ABB Traction) for third rail operation during 1992–1993. (*Kenneth C. Springirth photograph*)